# Jewish people

## understanding their world
### *sharing good news*

Randy Newman

thegoodbook
COMPANY

Engaging with Jewish People
© Randy Newman/The Good Book Company, 2016

Published by:
The Good Book Company

Tel (US): 866 244 2165
Tel (UK): 0333 123 0880
Email (US): info@thegoodbook.com
Email (UK): info@thegoodbook.co.uk

Websites:
North America: www.thegoodbook.com
UK: www.thegoodbook.co.uk
Australia: www.thegoodbook.com.au
New Zealand: www.thegoodbook.co.nz

ISBN: 9781784980528
Design by The Good Book Company / ninefootone creative
Printed in the UK

*Also in this series:*
- Engaging with Hindus
- Engaging with Atheists
- Engaging with Muslims

# Contents

# Engaging with...

# Preface

Christians have a wonderful message to tell the world. As the angel said at the birth of Jesus, it is "good news of great joy, *for all people*" (Luke 2 v 10). But sometimes we have been slow to take that message of forgiveness and new life to others.

Sometimes it's because we have become *distracted*. There are so many things that can push the need to tell others from its central place in our calling as individuals and churches. We get wrapped up in our own church issues, problems and politics. Or we get sidetracked by the very real needs of our broken and hurting world, and expend our energies dealing with the symptoms rather than the cause.

Sometimes it's because we have lacked *conviction*. We look at people who seem relatively happy or settled in their own beliefs, and just don't think Jesus is for them. Or perhaps we have forgotten just how good the good news is, and how serious the consequences for those who enter eternity unforgiven.

But often it has been *fear* that has held us back from sharing the good news about Jesus. When we meet people whose culture, background or beliefs are so different from ours, we can draw back from speaking about our own faith because we are afraid of saying the wrong thing, unintentionally offending them, or getting into an unhelpful argument that leads nowhere. Perhaps this is particularly so for sharing the good news of the Messiah with Jewish people.

This little series of books is designed to help with this last issue. We want to encourage Christian believers and whole churches to focus on our primary task of sharing the good news with the whole world. Each title aims to equip you with the understanding you need, so that you can build meaningful friendships with others from different backgrounds, and share the good news in a relevant and clear way.

It is our prayer that this book will help you do that with Jewish people wherever you meet them: a neighbor, friend or work colleague. They may have an active Jewish faith, or simply consider themselves Jewish because of their background and culture. We pray that the result would be "great joy" as they understand that Jesus really is their Messiah, and is good news for them.

*Tim Thornborough*
*Series Editor*

# Introduction

Writing this book brings me joy!

Allow me to begin by introducing you to a Yiddish word—*naches* (rhymes with "Loch Ness"). A dictionary would simply define it as "joy." But Yiddish is such a colorful language that mere definitions never fully convey the various nuances of a word. *Naches* has an element of pride to it, often because of the accomplishments of a child or a very close friend. If two old Jewish friends meet (which is the way many Jewish stories and jokes begin), one might say, "I have such *naches*! My eldest son just graduated from medical school."

Why do I begin a book about Jewish evangelism talking about *naches*? Because that's what I feel when I think that some of my Gentile brothers and sisters in Messiah want to learn how to share the good news of the Messiah with the Jewish people, my people. Truly, I'm overjoyed.

How could I not be? The gospel has brought such joy and meaning to my own life and I'm confident that you, the reader of this book, would say the same thing. I was born into a Jewish family in the suburbs of New York City at a time when "maintaining Jewish identity" was a high priority. My father fought in World War II, and my parents were of that generation that first learned of the horrors of the Holocaust, that demonic explosion that slaughtered one third of the world's Jewish population (6 out of 18 million). "Never again" became the slogan on every Jewish person's lips as they labored for the establishment of the state of Israel, a homeland and haven for the descendants of Abraham, Isaac, and Jacob. They also made sure their children attended additional "Hebrew School" to learn the basics of the faith and how to participate meaningfully in the traditions of worship that set us apart from other faiths.

Although my parents were not particularly observant in their practice or even believing in all that Judaism taught, they joined a Conservative synagogue that leaned toward the Orthodox variety, and made sure their three sons would have a *Bar Mitzvah* and not get assimilated into the predominantly "Christian" culture in which we lived.

Very soon, I learned we were not like Christians, and early on I learned that to be Jewish meant to be hated. I vividly recall being called "*kike*" and "*Christ-killer*" by "Christians" at my school. I remember my father receiving a request from our synagogue president to guard our congregation's property on a Halloween night. One year before, someone chose to carve a swastika into our synagogue lawn with a lawnmower.

I may not have been able to expound on all the major doctrines of Judaism but I knew, beyond a shadow of a doubt, that Jews do not believe in Jesus. For some reason, I took Judaism's spiritual aspects more seriously than the rest of my family. I continued to meet with our rabbi even after my *Bar Mitzvah*, which was far from typical. When I was 15 years old, I chose to diligently obey all the many commandments associated with the celebration of the holiest day of the Jewish calendar, *Yom Kippur*—the Day of Atonement. The traditions of the rabbis mandated that you fast on that day, not ride in a car, abstain from any work, and confess sins for the purpose of "afflicting one's soul." And so I walked to synagogue (about two miles from where we lived) and confessed every sin the liturgy listed. I had begun the holiday with the hopes that, if I obeyed all the commandments for that holiest of days, God would no longer seem distant and alien as he had up until that point.

But it didn't work. I walked home, watching the sun as it set, and felt no closer to God than I had 24 hours before. And then I looked down at my shoes. I was dressed in a suit and wore leather dress shoes to match the formal attire. At that moment, I remembered something I was taught back in Hebrew School years before—you don't wear leather shoes on *Yom Kippur*. If you were to visit a synagogue on *Yom Kippur*, you would see men dressed in fine suits and athletic shoes that don't match. It's a day for soft-soled footwear, not leather, which is equated with fine luxury—out of place on a day of repentance.

I wrestled with the notion that my shoes were the reason for my lack of connection with God. If only I had worn the right shoes, God wouldn't seem so alien to me, I reasoned. And then I thought, *"That's the stupidest thing in the world! Is that really what knowing God is all about? Wearing the right shoes? Obeying every obscure, demanding, rule the rabbis could concoct?"* If that was what a relationship with God was all about, I was not interested.

But still, I sensed there must be a better way and expressed some kind of prayer asking God to show me what it was. That began a process of searching that lasted more than five years. It included meeting a group of Christians who were different. They were different than me because they talked about having *"a personal relationship with God."* They were different than other "Christians" I knew because they challenged my thinking. They said that just because someone is gentile doesn't mean they are Christian. And they were different than most everyone I knew in that they talked *about* God and *to* God in a way I found tremendously attractive. I couldn't articulate it at the time but I was jealous that these *goyim* (a not-so-positive term for Gentiles) knew my Jewish God better than I did.

I began to read the Bible—both the so-called Old Testament and the New Testament—and found I had misunderstood both Judaism and Christianity. The God revealed in the *Tanach* (a Jewish term for the Law, the Prophets, and the Writings) was different than the rules-obsessed, law-enforcing deity I had heard about in Hebrew School. And the New Testament was not at all anti-Semitic as I had expected and been warned about. In fact, the New Testament sounded remarkably Jewish, quoting from David, Solomon, Hosea, Micah, and Malachi.

Most of all, I found that Jesus was not who I expected him to be—merely a good teacher. He made claims about himself that, if true, meant he was the Messiah and, if false, meant he was a megalomaniac. Best of all, I found this Jesus to be a delight to both my mind and my soul. He taught lessons that challenged and comforted, made sense and made for *shalom*—peace. He fulfilled what the prophets foretold and what my heart yearned for. And his death, I learned from Matthew, a Jewish man writing for a Jewish audience, atoned for sin in a way that no animal sacrifice in the temple or personal sacrifice after the temple's destruction could ever manage. He was the one Isaiah expected, the one Simeon hoped for, and the one I desperately wanted.

That same Jesus continues to amaze and delight me to this day. I regularly find ways in which he unifies the Old and New Testaments. He still challenges me with his teachings, cleanses me with his cross-work, and empowers me with his Spirit. He is the source of my every joy and the balm for my every *oy*. The thought of helping my Gentile brothers and sisters with the task of bringing the good news to my Jewish people cannot possibly bring anything but great happiness.

## Writing this book also makes me say "*Oy!*"

Here's another Yiddish word you might want to learn: *tsuris* (pronounced *TSOO-riss*, rhymes with absolutely nothing). The dictionary would say it means "trouble." Actually, it should be troubles, in the plural. Technically, there is a singular word, *tsureh*. But nobody ever uses that word because, *"how could there ever be only one problem? Give yourself time and you'll see things are worse than you thought."* We express *tsuris* by saying "*Oy*" (Oh!) or the more elaborate, "*Oy vey is meer*" (Oh, woe is me).

As soon as you put the word "Jewish" and the name "Jesus" together in a sentence, you're asking for *tsuris*. If there's one thing the vast majority of Jewish people believe, it's that "Jews don't believe in Jesus." In fact, they go further. If you "used to be Jewish" and you believe in Jesus, you're no longer Jewish, they insist. You betrayed and abandoned your people.

But wait! It gets worse. History gives Jewish people ample reason to resist the gospel. A great deal of hatred, persecution and worse has come to the Jewish people from Christians. Even after accounting for the fact that some of those people weren't really Christians, there still remains some terrible things said and done to my people by people I would have to call brothers or sisters in Christ.

It might be worth pausing at this point to explain something in the title of this book. If you're familiar with the series (*Engaging with Muslims, Engaging with Hindus*, etc.), you might have expected the title of this volume to be *Engaging with Jews*. But even the mere mention of the word "Jew" raises some problems. "Jew" was the word my people had to wear on an armband in Europe during the Holocaust to identify them as objects of hatred. The word "Jew" sounds harsh and hateful in the ears of many Jewish people. If you want to pave the way toward deeper friendship and more meaningful conversation with your Jewish friends, use the term "Jewish people" instead of the word "Jew."

I know. You want to say, *"But the New Testament calls them 'Jews.' If it's good enough for John and Paul, it's good enough for me."* But the New Testament was written before the Holocaust and before Martin Luther used that word in some pretty hateful ways. A minor vocabulary change can lead to major improvement in evangelism. I'll say more about word choices later. (And just to make this more tricky—it's not always bad to use the word "Jew." Thus, in this book, I will sometimes use that term. Is this consistent? No. But Jewish people tend to have a high tolerance for inconsistency.)

This all flows from the fact that the devil seems to hate the Jewish people. Just take a quick glance at our history and that statement doesn't seem far-fetched. To be sure, we could look at economic, sociological and historical factors that paved the way for the Nazis' engineering of "the final solution." But the extent of the evil, the dogged determination toward total annihilation of an entire race of people, and the fact that this wasn't the first time Jewish people faced this strategy (see Haman in the book of Esther, for example), points in the direction of demonic power, not just human obsessions. If indeed the Jewish people have a unique place in God's plan for the world, it does not seem odd that the devil has a place for them in his schemes as well.

Thus, engaging with Jewish people might not always be fun or easy or immediately fruitful. And if you get close to some Jewish people, Paul's "great sorrow and unceasing anguish" (Romans 9 v 2) that they do not know the One to whom all the law and the prophets point might resonate with you. But hopefully, you'll take heart from the fact that that same Paul used to persecute Jewish and Gentile followers of the One he eventually came to worship and proclaim. If God can knock a self-righteous Pharisee off his donkey on the way to Damascus, there is no limit to what he can do in and through the lives of the Jewish people he brings across your path.

## What this book is not

Not long ago, I spoke at a church's missions conference about the power of the gospel. I spoke of how good it is and how God has "blessed us in the heavenly realms with every spiritual blessing in Christ" (Ephesians 1 v 3). I wanted to motivate God's people to share good news out of a profound sense of gratitude for all God has done for rebellious sinners like us. I preached with the aim of having them take stock of the riches we have as blood-bought saints.

When I opened the session for questions, the first inquirer posed this question: *"So who do you think the 144,000 are in the book of Revelation?"*

My heart sank. And so did the questioner's when I fumferred for a minute and then said, *"I'm not really sure."* There are many questions we may have about future prophecy. Who are those 144,000? Who is the antichrist? Will Messiah's return come before a tribulation? Will he return before the millennium? This book will not answer those questions.

Nor will I be able to tackle the many theological questions about the relationship between Israel and the church, whether the political state of Israel is the fulfillment of prophecy, or what the best solutions are for the Israeli-Palestinian conflicts.

But please hear me carefully: I am not saying those questions are unimportant. They must be answered by every church and all individual believers. Just because God's people have not come to a consensus on these and many other questions does not mean we should fail to wrestle with them from the Scriptures by ignoring tricky passages. If you've ever heard a series of sermons on the book of Romans that skipped chapters 9, 10 and 11, you'll know why I'm concerned about this.

At points in this book, I'll give some suggestions about where I stand on certain debated issues. Whether you agree with my conclusions or not, I hope you'll dig into

God's word and decide for yourself what you believe about all that God teaches. I've suggested some resources that might help at the end of this book.

I do feel a need to offer a warning at this point. There may be times when you find my tone too lighthearted. I might even slip into a Yiddish expression or two that, given Yiddish's humorous nature, may seem flippant. (Did you catch that when I used the word "*fumfer*" a few paragraphs back. I didn't even realize that was Yiddish until my spell-checker went all *meshuguh*. There I go again.) I'm not just doing this to be funny. I want you to immerse yourself in the Jewish mindset that has learned to find humor just about anywhere. (Given our history, can you blame us?)

If you're going to engage with Jewish people, you might just need to lighten up a bit. Most Jewish people think Christians are uptight, humor-impaired and boring. That's a barrier to the gospel that we should demolish. In the midst of sharing good news with your Jewish friends, don't be afraid to crack a joke, laugh at yourself or smile. Like chicken soup, "it couldn't hurt."

## What this book is

My prayer for you as you read this book is that you will be encouraged. You will sense that the gospel reservoir from which you drink goes deeper than you had previously known. You will marvel more and more at how God's promises, prophecies and pictures in the early parts of his word have been fulfilled in the last part. You'll devote yourself to prayer for the salvation of the Jewish people, and you'll feel emboldened to start conversations that just might alter eternity.

God is as powerfully at work in the lives of Jewish people as he was when he parted the Red Sea. Their resistance or the evils done to them are not obstacles that can thwart the omnipotence of our God. In fact, friends of mine in Jewish missions tell me that Jewish people are more open to the gospel than ever. Perhaps that's because many Jewish people have defaulted to secularism long enough to discover its emptiness, shallowness and many disappointments. Or perhaps they've tried to reconnect (or connect for the first time) to the requirements of the law and found them crushing, as I did. Or perhaps they've come face to face with the failures of naïve Jewish optimism to bring about *shalom* in the Middle-East, or in racially strained cities, or in their own souls.

For whatever reason, Jewish people are reading the New Testament, talking about Jesus, visiting evangelistic websites, attending Christian Bible studies, sneaking in the back doors of churches and messianic congregations, and finding the One who has fulfilled the prophecies of Isaiah, Micah, Hosea and all the other prophets. Not only that—many of these Jewish people are embracing the One who satisfies their deepest longings, atones for all their sins, and grants them *naches* that will last for all eternity.

# Understanding Jewish people

# Chapter one

# Who are the Jewish people?

There are approximately 14 million Jewish people in our world of over 7 billion. That means my people make up less than one percent of the world's population. Actually it's a lot less than one percent. It's two tenths of one percent. And yet, in ways that could fill entire books, Jewish people have had a disproportionate amount of influence in the worlds of politics, education, business, science, entertainment, literature, and numerous other fields. When you consider how so very few (none?) of the world's other ancient peoples still exist (seen any Hittites or Jebusites lately?), you can see why some people see the hand of almighty God behind the people he calls "chosen."

A little less than half of those 14 million live in Israel. Almost that same number live in the United States with almost half of those living in or near New York City. Most Jewish people live in or near cities such as Los

Angeles, Paris, London, Toronto, Buenos Aries, and Moscow. Of course, by the time you read this, those locations may have shifted a bit. As I write this in early 2016, I hear about significant migrations of Jewish people from France to Israel because of rising anti-Semitism.

My people have always had to move because of hatred and persecution. Some of the numbers of change in population can stagger the imagination. Poland's demographics disturb the most. In 1930, 3 million Jewish people lived in Poland. Today there are barely 3,000. Most were killed by the Nazis. The rest escaped to America, Israel and elsewhere. The combined populations of Jewish people in Germany, Austria, Czechoslovakia, Hungary and Romania had grown to over 2.5 million by 1930. Today, those locations account for less than 200,000.

Of course, these numbers all presume it's easy to identify who is Jewish and who is not. They're the biological descendants of Abraham, Isaac and Jacob, right? But such simplicity rarely occurs in the Jewish world. In fact, you could read lengthy discussions about "Who is a Jew?" that would make you wonder if you've stumbled into a law-school classroom or a Shakespearean tragedy.

Part of the problem developed when the newly established nation of Israel passed "the law of return." This allowed Jewish people from all over the world to settle in Israel and claim automatic citizenship *"if they identify themselves as Jewish."* You see the potential problems, don't you? The Israeli government had to qualify that a bit. Eventually they landed on the view that you were Jewish if your mother was Jewish. Why your mother and not your father, since so many places in the Scriptures trace people's ancestries through the line of the father? Because the centuries of persecution often included the raping of Jewish women by non-Jewish oppressors. This led to births of children who knew who their mother was but for whom identifying their father wasn't so easy. So the rabbis decided that the way to keep our people intact and distinguish who "we" are from who "they" are was to keep track of the mothers and their children. God did raise up fathers to lead the families and communities from the survivors of such cruelty, but it all made for a rather messy situation. Perhaps this is why Jewish people now place such a high priority on the family. Then again, the Bible values the family rather highly as well.

For the purpose of this book, however, we don't need to explore the debate about "Who is a Jew?" any further. The Jewish people you're likely to meet won't be wondering if they're really Jewish. They'll either identify themselves as such or not. Some, to be sure, may be wondering what that means. They may not have been raised in a very observant family and now they would like to connect to their roots. In fact, a growing number of Jewish people in America are reclaiming or re-establishing or finding for the first time their Jewish roots during their middle age. These kinds of newfound identities could be fertile soil in which to cultivate conversations about the Messiah. But I'm getting ahead of myself. Let's wait a bit before we explore how we reach out.

For now, it's worth reflecting further on understanding who we're talking to. Jewish people love to point out that Judaism is more than a religion. And it's more than a race. And it's more than an ethnicity. Some like to say,

*"It's a way of life."* Jewish people weave together doctrine, diet, humor, tone of voice, and a dozen other aspects of life all under the banner of "Jewish." Part of the reason why Jewish evangelism is so difficult is that most Jewish people see Christianity as so alien. Being Jewish is not just having a different set of beliefs. It's different flavors of food, different ways to tell jokes, different views about politics, and different planets of social customs. If I had to condense what it means to be Jewish to four prevailing themes, I'd say they're pain, pride, pleasure, and promise.

## Pain

I've already mentioned enough things to highlight the reality of pain in the Jewish mindset. A fair number of Jewish holidays commemorate times when enemies tried to wipe us out but God spared us. For Passover we remember our deliverance from slavery to the Egyptians with a feast called a *seder*. For *Purim*, we rejoice that wicked Haman's plot to kill us didn't succeed and we nosh on cookies called *hamantaschen*. For *Hanukkah*, we dedicate ourselves to God, who empowered us to retake the temple from Antiochus Epiphanies, and we eat potato pancakes. One Jewish comic quipped that most of our holidays could be summarized with three short sentences: *"They tried to kill us. We won. Let's eat."*

## Pride

Because we have survived so much, against such odds, so many times, we have developed a kind of Jewish pride that has been, in my opinion, both a blessing and a curse. It's a blessing because it builds upon itself. It looks at past accomplishments and spurs us on to even greater ones. Not only do we survive persecutions but we also produce Nobel Prize winners, cure diseases, write master-pieces, advance social improvements, and rise above our circumstances. We can do anything—or so we think. This kind of pride has enabled the country of Israel to thrive economically and agriculturally even though it consists largely of desert. The Jewish people have developed a will to excel even when the odds are against them. When Jewish people reflect on their corporate rags-to-riches status, they grow more energized to excel still more.

But ethnic pride has also been a curse because, along the way, some Jewish people have forgotten God. Despite warnings like the one in Deuteronomy 8, it is easy to think we are the source of our success instead of appreciating the gracious hand of God. Through Moses, God warned:

> Be careful that you do not forget the LORD your God ... Otherwise, when you eat and are satisfied ... then your heart will become proud and you will forget the LORD your God, who brought you out of Egypt, out of the land of slavery.
>
> **Deuteronomy 8 v 11-14**

This warning is for all of us, whether Jewish or Gentile. Everyone must be wary of a reliance on self that forgets our constant dependence on the One who gives us every breath, step and thought. Without him, we cease to exist—both individually as persons and corporately as a people.

For some, this ethnic pride has theological roots—but not ones that accurately reflect the teaching of Scripture. God's word goes out of its way to say that God did not choose the nation of Israel because of any merit of its own.

> The LORD did not set his affection on you and choose you because you were more numerous than other peoples, for you were the fewest of all peoples. But it was because the LORD loved you and kept the oath he swore to your ancestors that he brought you out with a mighty hand and redeemed you from the land of slavery, from the power of Pharaoh king of Egypt. **Deuteronomy 7 v 7-8**

Tragically, for some, this pride has angry roots. I have interacted with enough Jewish people to hear a recurring theme of resentment that God didn't prevent or stop the Holocaust and other evils. For these people, their success, especially the establishment, protection, and prosperity of the nation of Israel has been *in spite of God* rather than *because of him*. Their cry of "Never again!" means that they will prevent another Holocaust by fighting to the death to provide a safe haven for Jewish people in Israel—even if God doesn't come through for them. I write these words with tears and an ache in my heart but I know these sentiments are real for at least some of my people.

If you're tempted to think condemning thoughts right now about Jewish pride, consider the universal and insidious nature of pride. And reflect carefully that you too may, from time to time, take credit for things that actually come from the hand of our gracious God. Examine your heart and see if you harbor any bitterness toward God for not always behaving the way you want him to. Spend time considering how necessary the cross was to atone for your sins, and drink deeply from the well of gospel grace that chose to rescue you from your own self-reliance. And then ask God to give you the same burden for the Jewish people that Paul had, agreeing with his description of them as...

zealous for God, but their zeal is not based on knowledge. Since they did not know the righteousness of God and sought to establish their own, they did not submit to God's righteousness.  **Romans 10 v 2-4**

## Pleasure

I've already mentioned the close ties between Jewish holidays and food. But deliciousness is not just for ceremonial occasions. Who needs to wait for a wedding or a holiday to enjoy lean corned beef, fresh gefilte fish, stuffed cabbage, bagels, cream cheese and lox, or a dessert tray that'll warrant a lecture from a cardiologist? And this goes beyond the calendar. It shapes a whole way of seeing. Many Jewish people see Gentile culture (which they do not distinguish from Christianity) as sterile, bland, and in desperate need of a new caterer. Such realities are not insignificant when it comes to reaching out with the gospel.

I've also mentioned our love for humor. We love to laugh and make others laugh. For many years, the stand-up comedy world was dominated by Jewish comedians. Perhaps we're trying to counter our many years of trouble and sorrow. Or perhaps our times of lack propel us to go after more and more. I'll save it for the cultural anthropologists to analyze the causes. For the sake of this book, I want you to see that Jewish people like nice things, appreciate good music and art, love to celebrate with food and laughter, and think that life—this life—is a good thing. We don't just sing "L'Chaim" ("To Life!") because it was a nice show-tune in *Fiddler on the Roof*. That song was written for the musical because it reflects how Jewish people think and live. If you're going to engage well with Jewish people, you'll want to show and tell how the gospel is good news for this life as well as for the next. And you should probably do so over a nice meal.

## Promise

The Jewish mindset, at its best, looks simultaneously backwards and forwards. For example, every year at Passover we retell the story of God's miraculous deliverance of his people from slavery. Long ago he worked miracles to pour out judgment on Egypt's false gods through the ten plagues, and displayed his power by parting the Red Sea. But we also look forward during that celebration to the time when all slavery, all oppression, all idolatry, and all wickedness will be wiped away. We end every *Seder* (Passover meal) with the words, *"Next year in Jerusalem,"* a shorthand reference to the time when the Messiah comes to set up his kingdom on earth.

Thus, Judaism has a forward-looking posture to it, even for some of the most secularized, non-observant Jews. And that future orientation has a strong aspect of hope to it. In fact, the Israeli national anthem is called "HaTikvah", which means "The Hope"! Perhaps this is why Jewish people involve themselves in politics or pursue civic causes. There's something in the Judaic DNA that longs for a better day when people "will beat their swords into plowshares and their spears into pruning hooks" (Isaiah 2 v 4). For some of them, this taints their view of Christians who they see as only interested in life after death, only in heaven and not caring about earth, and "so heavenly minded as to be no earthly good." Part of the task in proclaiming the gospel to Jewish people involves agreement that things are not as they should be while still pointing to eternity—the only time when all longings for heaven can be fulfilled.

As followers of the Messiah and lovers of all of the Scriptures, both Old and New Testaments, we see even greater reasons for hope and looking forward. God has already sent his Messiah once, so we are confident that he'll send him again to fulfill all remaining prophecies. In the meantime, the promises of Romans 11 tell us that God is not finished with the Jewish people.

I ask, then: Did God reject his people? By no means! **Romans 11 v 1**

This verse answers Paul's rhetorical question with a re-sounding "No!" Israel did not "stumble so as to fall beyond recovery (v 11)." The Bible gives us good reason to be optimistic about fruitfulness in proclaiming the good news to the Jewish people.

God promised Abraham that his descendants would be as numerous as the stars in the sky, and that they will be a light to the Gentiles. Some interpreters believe that Messianic Jews will bring ultimate fulfillment to that promise when they, as followers of Jesus, will join all the proclaimers of the gospel, tell of the One who is "the light of the world," and play important roles in the fulfillment of the great commission. Whatever the detail, we should be encouraged that God has not rejected our Jewish friends and neighbours, and that sharing the gospel with them is not a fruitless exercise. There will be many Jewish believers in the Messiah in the crowd who gather around the Lion of the tribe of Judah, singing his praise forever (see Revelation 5 v 5-13). Perhaps one of the Jewish people you know will be among them.

### Watch Your Language

Words do more than just convey meaning. They paint pictures, express emotions, and stimulate responses. Some words offend or sound harsh or prompt pain. You can avoid unnecessary stumbling blocks by choosing certain words instead of others.

Say "Jewish people" instead of "Jews."

Say "Messiah" instead of "Christ."

It's OK to say "Jesus" but you might want to also use "Yeshua." Don't be surprised if you need to explain who you're talking about.

Say "believer in Jesus" instead of "Christian." It's also good to sometimes distinguish "Jewish believers in Jesus" and "Gentile believers in Jesus."

"Congregation" is better than "church."

Avoid the words "missionary" and "missions."

And if you're *farblondget*—hopelessly lost and confused—by the different terms and types of Jewish religion, don't worry; there's a glossary of terms over the page.

# Naomi's story

Naomi grew up in a very observant Jewish home, the daughter of a rabbi of a Conservative congregation. She knew Judaism well, both from her family's practice of rituals in the home and from the teaching in her Jewish schools. So, when Tabitha, her Christian babysitter began to talk to her about Jesus, Naomi's rejection was emphatic. *"No, Jesus is not real. I'll never believe in him."* Even as a young child she challenged her babysitter with questions, like, *"If you believe in Jesus, isn't that idolatry because it's believing in more than one god?"*

Still, even though she had arguments against what her babysitter said, what Naomi couldn't debate was that Tabitha was loving, confident and served her whole family with a sacrificial heart. Eventually, both parents embraced her as another member of the family. Even to this day, after almost two decades of serving as far more than just a babysitter, Tabitha continues to stay close to Naomi and her family. Much of her witness was indirect. She showed Naomi movies about Jesus' birth and his death, and spoke of Paul's conversion and other New Testament stories, but they all seemed *"out of context for me."* But something drew Naomi in ways that her Jewish practices did not. Somehow all the lighting of candles, reciting of prayers, and eating of ceremonial foods seemed like just "mere ritual."

Intriguingly, while Naomi argued against belief in Jesus, inwardly she began to wonder: *Could he be the Messiah? Did he rise from the dead? Did he fulfill prophecy?* The person of Jesus, displayed through the gentleness of Tabitha, moved Naomi closer and closer to belief. But it was a belief she resisted fiercely. *"I pushed those thoughts away a lot. I didn't want Christianity to be part of my life. I was so against it. I didn't want Jesus at all!"*

Then, one day in ninth grade, an unwitting evangelist

helped Naomi cross over from darkness to light. In her Jewish school, taught exclusively by strict adherents of Judaism, Naomi found herself defending Jesus—not out loud but undeniably in her head. Naomi's history teacher presented a lecture on why Jews don't believe in Jesus. She was "hard core" in her efforts to disprove Christianity, insisting that no one—Jewish or Gentile—should believe in the resurrection. She presented "proofs" and "evidence" and "facts" that it "couldn't happen."

But, Naomi says, *"It had the complete opposite effect on me. She convinced me that Jesus did rise from the dead! In that moment, I knew I believed."* She went home from school and immediately told Tabitha that she believed and wanted to read the New Testament and learn all she could about Jesus. Over the next few days, as she read the New Testament, Naomi sensed that, *"It completed every question I had my entire life."*

To this day, over five years after that eternity-changing day in her Jewish school, Naomi delights in how meaningful and joyful it is to believe in Jesus. *"I finally decided to trust my life to Jesus for his forgiveness, and I received new life through the power of God's Holy Spirit."*

**Reflection**

- What are you hoping to gain from reading this book?

- What fears do you have about speaking, and perhaps sharing the gospel, with someone from a Jewish background?

- Where do you come into contact with Jewish people on a daily or occasional basis? What are the different possibilities for having a conversation and perhaps starting a friendship?

## Glossary of useful terms

**Bar Mitzvah/Bat Mitzvah.** A ceremony for 13-year-old boys (Bar Mitzvah) and girls (Bat Mitzvah) as they become "adult" participants in the liturgies of Judaism.

**Evangelism.** The verbal proclamation of the unique message that Jesus, the Messiah, died to save sinners. Many other messages may pave the way for that message (pre-evangelism) or build support for that message (apologetics).

**Gentile.** A non-Jewish person; anyone who is not a physical descendant of Abraham, Isaac, and Jacob, regardless of belief.

**Gospel.** The verbal message that God sent his Son, Jesus, to die as a sacrifice for sins so that those who trust in him will have eternal life.

**Hebrew.** The language that most of the Old Testament was written in and is still spoken today by many Jewish people.

**Holocaust.** The horrific, systematic killing of 6 million Jewish people and many others by the Nazis in the 1940s.

**Jewish.** The general term for many things, including religion, culture and ethnicity related to the Jewish people, those who are physically descended from Abraham, Isaac, and Jacob.

**Judaism.** The faith system derived from the Old Testament and other Jewish writings that is practiced by and influences of the Jewish people.

**Messiah.** The person promised by numerous prophecies in the Old Testament who atones for sin and establishes God's kingdom of righteousness, justice and peace.

**Messianic.** An adjective describing any of the many

things associated with the coming of the Messiah.

**Passover.** The holiday that retells and celebrates God's deliverance from slavery in Egypt.

**Rabbi.** A spiritual leader in a synagogue or Jewish community.

**Seder.** The ceremonial meal of the holiday of Passover, the remembrance of God's deliverance from slavery in Egypt, as recounted in the book of Exodus.

**Shalom.** The Hebrew word that means peace (and many other things that flow from that peace—individual well-being, social harmony, a sense of wholeness, restoration of damaged things, etc.).

**Synagogue.** The place for most Jewish corporate worship times or celebrations.

**Talmud.** A collection of Jewish discussions and commentaries on various parts of the Bible. Some terms associated with parts of the Talmud include Gemara, Mishnah and Midrash.

**Tanach.** A Hebrew acrostic term for the parts of the 39 books of the Old Testament: Law, Prophets, Writings.

**Torah.** The first five books of the Bible: Genesis, Exodus, Leviticus, Numbers, and Deuteronomy.

**Yiddish.** A language developed by Jewish people in Eastern Europe who wove together elements of Hebrew, German and other languages.

# Chapter two

# What do Jewish people believe?

## 1. What you might *think* Jewish people believe

Many Christians discover a sizeable gap between what they expect Jewish people to believe and what they actually do believe. They think their Jewish neighbors, friends, or co-workers will act like the Israelites they read about in the Old Testament or the Pharisees they encounter in the Gospels. Neither picture resembles the people they meet today. When they actually engage in conversation with real live *actual* Jewish people, Christians are frequently surprised at how unlearned Jews are about "their" scriptures, or how secularly they think about life, or how unconcerned they are about God, religion or anything eternal. Numerous theories have been suggested as to why this is the case. For our purposes, we need not know why this is true. We just need to expect that, more often than not, it *will* be true.

It will not help a great deal if you find out which variety of synagogue they attend (Orthodox, Conservative, Reform, Reconstructionist, or other) and assume they adhere to all that their rabbi teaches. In fact, their rabbi might not adhere to all that is implied by his synagogue label of "Orthodox" or "Conservative," etc. It's just not that neat. Christians have denominations such as Presbyterian, Baptist, Methodist, etc. which are also not as clearly cut as they once were. The distinctions between Orthodox, Conservative, Reform and other types of Jewish congregations are not as precise as we might expect or want.

To be sure, we can expect a general spectrum from Orthodox on the conservative end to Reform on the liberal end. But already we have some confusion, don't we? A Conservative synagogue lands somewhere in the middle. And I do mean "somewhere." Some Conservative synagogues are far more "conservative" than others. Generally speaking, Jewish people who call themselves orthodox will emphasize obedience to the commandments in the Torah and will seem more devoted or observant. You might think of them as the fundamentalists of the faith. Reform Jews, toward the other end of the spectrum, will emphasize Jewish identity, affiliation with a nationality, and will not insist upon observance of too many rituals. You might think of them as the liberals of the faith. Of course, you should not think of conservative or liberal in political terms. The vast majority of American Jewish people are politically liberal even if they are ultra-orthodox in their practice. I told you it was complicated.

Conservative Jews land in the middle when it comes to how much of the commandments they adhere to and how much they allow for accommodation to modern cultural trends. Reconstructionists, a recently developed group, are more concerned with the Jewish people and culture than with religion and God. Thus, it's hard to put them on the spectrum at all.

We could go on and on about the distinctions, history, trends, etc. of the varieties of Jewish expression and practice. But that would not help you a great deal with reaching out with the gospel. What you want to do is talk to individual Jewish people and try to understand *their* understanding of Judaism and *their* practices and values. Even if a Jewish friend were to tell you he was part of an Orthodox synagogue, you still might not know much about his own beliefs. Ask questions, seek understanding, allow for inconsistencies, probe to find out how they arrived at their current beliefs, and forget about "pigeon-holing" anyone into any pre-constructed categories. Most likely, they will not be offended if you ask in a spirit of friendly enquiry.

My grandfather faithfully attended worship services every Friday evening and every Saturday morning at the Orthodox synagogue in his neighborhood, but once told me he didn't believe in God! *"How could anyone believe in a god who would allow the Holocaust?"* he once told me. When I asked him why he still went to synagogue, he looked at me with a puzzled look, shrugged his shoulders, and said, *"Because I'm Jewish!"*

## 2. What Jewish people *actually do* believe
**Joke:** Ask two Jewish people a question, and you'll get at least four answers.

Given what I've already written about the diversity within the Jewish world and the tendency of Jewish people towards secularism, it might seem absurd to try to cover "What Jewish people believe." But here are some important things to know about what Jewish people tend to believe about God, people, life after death, and ultimately important things. I'll save the discussion of what they think about Jesus, Christianity and Christians for the next section. But remember, the most important thing is what the specific Jewish person you're talking to believes.

## Two revelations

One place to start in understanding what and how Jewish people think is to grasp that Jewish tradition has believed in **two revelations** from God. On Mount Sinai, God revealed his **written word to Moses** and tasked him with the responsibility of getting it written down. But he gave an **oral revelation**—one to be passed on by word of mouth. Thus, rabbis speak of the written law and the oral law.

At its best, this idea allows for the fact that human beings take in information in many ways—not just through reading or our intellect. We also learn and grow by hearing. By extension, it could be surmised that we also benefit from seeing beauty, hearing music, eating food, laughing at jokes, spending time with family—and the list could go on seemingly forever. Perhaps we can see parallels with what Christian theologians have termed God's written revelation (found only in the Bible) and his general revelation (found in nature, reason, beauty, etc.).

But as you might guess, this belief in two revelations can result in many problems. How do you protect the accuracy of oral tradition? Ultimately, the oral revelation did get written down as the *Talmud,* consisting of the *Gemara* or the *Midrash* or the *Mishna* or combinations of two or more of these or other writings. But this raises other questions. What happens if something in the oral tradition contradicts something in the written tradition? Does one hold a higher authority?

In other words, regarding revelation or "how we know what we know," for Jewish people, it's a combination of divine revelation and human reason. Thus, Jewish people have always placed a high value on education, thinking and deep reflection. The Jewish style of education involves a great deal of arguing, in the good sense of that word. You can better understand your point of view if you can also argue for the opposing point of view. That's why so many lawyers come from Jewish backgrounds. We have a long tradition of saying, *"On the one hand, it's this. But on the other hand, it's that."*

Perhaps that explains why many Jewish people hold theological views which contradict what the Scriptures clearly teach. Their emphasis on human reason sets them up to see the Bible as something that can evolve or be reinterpreted or adapted in almost infinite ways. On a campus where I serve as a campus minister, I saw a poster promoting the Jewish Student Association. The top of the poster said, *"What's Your And?"* It then listed options:

"Proud to be Jewish and Asian"
"Proud to be Jewish and a Geek"

"Proud to be Jewish and Greek"
"Proud to be Jewish and Gay"
"Proud to be Jewish and American"

I'm guessing that *"Proud to be Jewish and a believer in Jesus"* wouldn't fit.

Even with all this diversity and inconsistency, we can expect most Jewish people will believe the following about three major topics:

## 1. God

**God does exist and he's worthy of worship.** He's almighty, all-knowing, and good. Most of all, he's holy—so holy, in fact, that his name is to be treated with extreme reverence. That's why many Jewish people will not write the word God or Lord. Instead, they'll write G-d or L-rd. Writing the name runs the risk of "taking it in vain." In a similar way, many Jewish people use indirect ways to refer to "the holy One, blessed be he." A common circumlocution is "The name." You may hear someone with even only a small amount of knowledge of the Hebrew language say, *"Baruch HaShem"* which literally means, "Bless the name." It's an indirect way of saying, "Praise the Lord." (In fact, many Jewish people may feel quite uncomfortable when they hear Christians speak so casually about God and sprinkle ordinary speech with "Praise the Lord.")

One thing Jewish people believe for sure is that "God is one," as stated in the central prayer of Judaism, the *Shema*, (the Hebrew word for "hear"—with the emphasis on the second syllable; *shuh MA*, not *SHEE ma*) from Deuteronomy 6 v 4-6. "Hear, O Israel: the L-RD our G-d, the L-RD is one." Here is the crux of Judaism's rejection of Christianity. They think Christians believe in three gods. That's not only wrong but horribly, offensively, blasphemously wrong. I'll say more on how to address this in the second section of the book.

## 2. People
**People are basically good**, capable of great accomplishments, and only slightly tainted by sin. In fact, the problem of sin does not loom large in modern Judaism the way it does for Christians. To be sure, you should repent on *Yom Kippur*, the Day of Atonement. But let's not get carried away. People, especially the Jewish people, are the main contributors to the improvement of the world and we shouldn't cripple our potential through an overemphasis on sin. As the writer Chaim Potok put it in his history of the Jewish people, *Wanderings*, *"For some mysterious reason, God's world was imperfect. Man's task was to help God perfect it."*[1]

## 3. Eternity
**What happens after we die is something we'll find out then and we shouldn't be so concerned about it prematurely.** The Bible, they would say, does not emphasize heaven, the afterlife, eternity, or even salvation. So neither should we. That would distract us from the task

---

1 Chaim Potok, *Wanderings: Chaim Potok's History of the Jews*. Alfred A Knopf. New York, NY (1979), page xiii.

of making this world a better place. *Tikkun* magazine, a popular and influential journal in and beyond the Jewish world, exemplifies this vision in their mission statement, "to heal, repair, and transform the world."

In the midst of all this discussion of theology, don't forget that Jewish people tend to take life in a lighthearted way. In the midst of serious theological discussion, they'll insert a joke or a story and freely admit that they're inconsistent or confused. For Jewish people, this is entirely proper and certainly not a problem. For many Christian people this seems bothersome and disrespectful.

For example, in the beginning of a rather serious book about searching for God, Jewish author Eric Weiner writes:

> I blame my confusion, as I do most things, on my parents. I was raised in a secular household where God's name was uttered only when someone stubbed their toe ... or ate something especially delicious ... We were gastronomical Jews ... If we could eat it then it was Jewish and, by extension, had something to do with God. As far as I was concerned, God resided not in Heaven or the Great Void but in the Frigidaire, somewhere between the cream cheese and the salad dressing. We believed in an edible deity, and that was about the extent of our spiritual life.[1]

---

1 Eric Weiner, *Man Seeks God: My Flirtations with the Divine*. Twelve. New York, NY (2012), page 4.

### 3. What Jewish people believe about Jesus, Christianity and Christians

Before understanding what Jewish people believe about Jesus, Christianity and Christians, you need to feel why they hold these convictions. It's not simply a case of misinformation. It's a tragic story of pain, anti-Semitism, lies and evil. Again, if God holds a special place in his plan for the Jewish people, so does the devil. And our adversary has done a masterful job of distorting the gospel so that Jewish people think it's ridiculous (at best) or downright disgusting (at worst). The walls against the gospel consist of both intellectual boulders and emotional concrete.

I won't attempt a lengthy analysis of why some Christians have thought and said false, hateful, disturbing things about the Jewish people. Some have suggested that, because the Jewish people rejected the Messiah when he came, God has given up on them and we should too. (No one says it so crassly but that may be the conviction at the bottom of their thoughts.) First of all, that idea is not based on fact. Some Jewish people did accept Jesus as the Messiah when he came. In fact, the majority of his first followers were Jewish. Second, if God "gave up on" people who, at first, don't respond to him, we'd all be lost—forever. Moishe Rosen, the founder of Jews for Jesus, was once asked to comment on the notion that perhaps God's plans for Israel no longer apply to them because they rejected God. He said, *"My people have rejected God? So what else is new?"*

I will simply offer a few samples and suggest that when you talk to Jewish people about Jesus, the temperature in the room may go up by a dozen degrees or so. The symbol of the cross, so dear to many Christians, makes the hairs on the back of many Jewish heads stand up in anger. Consider what Martin Luther once wrote, toward the end of his life. Perhaps he was frustrated that Jewish people didn't respond to the gospel in his day as much as he had hoped:

> First, their synagogues should be set on fire ... Secondly, their homes should likewise be broken down and destroyed ... Thirdly, they should be deprived of their prayer-books and Talmuds ... Fourthly, their rabbis must be forbidden under threat of death to teach any more.[1]

I'll stop there. He added several more points and poured out a lot more hate. Luther wasn't the first to say such things. Here's some of what John Chrysostom, a Christian leader in the fourth century, declared:

> The synagogue is worse than a brothel ... it is the den of scoundrels and the repair of wild beasts ... the temple of demons devoted to idolatrous cults ... the refuge of brigands and debauchees, and the cavern of devils ... I would say the same things about their souls ... As for me, I hate the synagogue ... I hate the Jews for the same reason.[2]

Michael Brown, who has done extensive research about

---

1  Martin Luther, *Concerning the Jews and Their Lies*, in Talmage, *Disputation and Dialogue*, Ktav Publications (1975), pages 34-36.

2  Quoted in Malcolm Hay, *The Roots of Christian Anti-Semitism*, New York: Liberty Press (1981), pages 27-28.

this painful topic, concludes, *"Sadly and to our shame, we could go on and on with sickening quotation after quotation, with example after example of bitter Jew-hatred among the leaders of the 'Church'... The Church has blood on her hands."*

You might be tempted to think that such foolish talk comes from the mouths of people who really were not true followers of Jesus. True, the nature of Christian faith is that you can think you're a Christian when you're really fooling yourself. Jesus did indeed say that some who have called him "Lord, Lord" will hear the response, "I never knew you."

But questioning Martin Luther's salvation doesn't sound like a good idea to me. I think he really was saved. But he thought and said terrible things about the Jewish people. Luther wasn't inerrant. The Bible he preached was. And that Bible tells us to seek the truth, proclaim it in love, and ask God to penetrate through barriers erected by evil, pain and sin. Nothing is impenetrable for the God of Abraham, Isaac and Jacob—even walls of resentment by stiff-necked people who have been persecuted by other stiff-necked people.

One episode in history may serve to illustrate some of the antipathy between Jews and Christians. At the time of Jesus' visitation to our world, the Jewish people consisted of many factions (another opportunity to say, *"So what else is new?"*). **Pharisees** saw themselves as the keepers of the law. **Sadducees** denied key tenets, such as the resurrection of the dead, but still saw themselves as part of the people of Israel. The **Essenes** retreated to the desert of Qumran and lived secluded lives. The **Zealots** pursued power politics against Rome. After Jesus' resurrection, some Jewish followers of his came to be known as **Nazarenes** and enjoyed a certain amount of insider status within the multifaceted Jewish world of their day.

Things became strained when the Romans destroyed the temple in AD 70. Those who believed Jesus' prophetic words to be about that traumatic event ran away to protect themselves (see Luke 21 v 21) rather than stay and fight in a losing cause. The surviving Jews (who did not accept Jesus as Messiah) resented his followers and deemed them "traitors."

Less than 70 years later, a similar event widened the split even further. Simon Bar Kochba, a military figure, organized a revolt against Rome. The leading rabbi of the time, Akiva, declared Bar Kochba to be the Messiah. Most of the Jewish world rallied behind Akiva and Bar Kochba to finally end the oppression of Rome. But Jewish believers in Jesus could not sign on. The Messiah had already come, they insisted. The revolt failed, Bar Kochba and Akiva were killed, and the "Nazarenes" were now condemned as the worst form of traitors.

The Jewish people you meet today may know absolutely nothing about Bar Kochba. They don't have to. The distrust between Jews and Gentiles runs deep—far beyond memory or cognition. Your asking them to "join" Christianity may seem as alien or as distasteful as asking them to join a local neo-Nazi party. No wonder Jewish people don't even want to refer to dates as BC or AD. They don't think "Before Christ" or "in the year of our Lord" should demarcate history. He's not their "Lord." Thus, they refer to dates as either BCE ("before the common era") or CE ("in the common era"). Insisting that they adopt your terms for chronology doesn't seem like a good battle to fight in the larger discussion of who Jesus was and why he came.

## The Messiah

You may have noticed in the previous section about what Jewish people actually do believe that nothing was mentioned about the Messiah. For most of them, the Messiah just isn't a big deal. Granted, he should be. And part of the task of Jewish evangelism is trying to point that out. But for most Jewish people today, the notion of a personal Messiah just doesn't make sense. If anything, there may be a messianic age in the future when there will be peace on earth. Or, as some hold, the "Messiah" is not a person but the collective entity of the nation of Israel.

But many Jewish people have grown weary of holding out hope. So the less they think about a Messiah, a messianic age, or the potential for Israel to transform the world, the better. We shouldn't grow weary of pointing out how often the Scriptures mention, allude to, or predict an individual Messiah. We just shouldn't be surprised if this sounds like startling news.

There are some common misconceptions about the Christian faith that we would be wise to correct. We should do so with gentleness and respect but with firm conviction that some beliefs are wrong no matter how widespread they may be. For reasons that should now be obvious, a huge "we-they" mentality exists for Jewish people. And "they" have all tried to kill "us." Thus, Jewish people tend to think of all Gentiles as Christians. All Gentiles—you, the funny-haired preacher on television,

Billy Graham, the Nazis and that weird guy who stands on the street corner waving his Bible in the air—are all "Christians."

A strategic moment in Jewish evangelism occurs when a Christian shows the difference between Gentiles and Christians. Gentiles are non-Jews. Christians are born-again believers in Jesus. Another way of understanding this is that Judaism is a religion you're born into. Christianity is not. You must be born again into Christianity. This is an alien concept to most Jewish people, and it may take numerous restatements before it sinks in.

Similarly, many Jewish people think that Roman Catholicism is the standard expression of Christianity in the world today. Thus, whatever the Pope has recently said is considered universally accepted by all "Christians." The result is that some of the distinct emphases of Roman Catholicism, taken to be central pillars of Christianity, seem particularly odd to Jewish ways of thinking.

For example, the insistence on celibate clergy or an overemphasis on virginity seems like a disdain for sex, which Jewish people find bizarre. They're repulsed by this caricature of Christianity, not just in disagreement with it. You don't need to deliver a lecture on church history, recount all the reasons for the Protestant Reformation, or state why John Calvin's your guy in order to distance yourself from this false perception. A simple, *"Well, not all Christians agree with the Roman Catholic expression of the faith"* may suffice.

Finally, most Jewish people know very, very little about Jesus. They think they know about him—but their view of him is far from what we read in the New Testament.

In fact, they may say, *"I think Jesus was great. I just don't like his followers."* As I once believed, they think Jesus was a good rabbi who said some nice things about love and peace. But he certainly wasn't God or the messiah or anything more than a very good teacher and, perhaps, a prophet. Our task is to introduce them to the real Jesus revealed in the Gospels, not the one they've created in their own imaginations. Many Jewish believers say that, when they first read Matthew, Mark, Luke, or John (or all four of them), they were surprised and amazed by the Jesus they met—surprised at how different he was from the Jesus they were told about, and amazed at how attractive, brilliant, bold, powerful and divine he was.

## 4. What Jewish people *must* believe

So far, I have simply assumed you think Jewish people must believe in Jesus to be saved. I certainly hope you do. But you would not be the first Christian to start to doubt that as you get close to Jewish people or see how moral they are, or suspect how sincere they are, or observe how their religion is so very close to yours. After all, they read the same Bible you do. They just stop short. And when you grow in your understanding of how persecuted they've been, especially by people who call themselves Christians, you may be tempted to wonder if, just perhaps, God may have a separate plan for the salvation of the Jews—one that doesn't include Jesus, the one whose name has become so repulsive to them.

You might hear some Christian leaders talk about the Jews as "our older brothers" or "God's chosen people" and conclude that there must be some kind of "two-covenant system"—one for the Jews and one for everyone else. But I hope you'll "take every thought captive" and think deeply about what the Scriptures have to say about the need of Jewish people for Jesus. I also hope you'll come to see that Judaism on its own basis, with its own Scriptures, points to, requires, and longs for a Messiah who atones for sin as the only way of salvation, for all people—both Jews and Gentiles. Moses looked for another prophet like himself, but who would be so much greater than Moses (Deuteronomy 18 v 14-20). And the prophets looked forward to another system that points to a new and better way of relating to God (Ezekiel 36 v 26-27).

An extensive case could certainly be made from the New Testament about the need of Jewish people's to believe in Jesus as their Messiah. For the scope of this book, I will limit my comments to two crucial verses:

> I am not ashamed of the gospel, because it is the power of God for the salvation of everyone who believes: first for the Jew, then for the Gentile. For in the gospel a righteousness from God is revealed, a righteousness that is by faith from first to last, just as it is written: "The righteous will live by faith."
>
> **Romans 1 v 16-17**

Note that this verse is both universal, but also very specific. The gospel is offered to "everyone", both Jews and Gentiles. But it requires the particular response of "belief." Note also that Paul emphasizes the gospel's power. Given what follows in Romans, it is clear that only the gospel has this power for salvation. No amount of self-produced righteousness, whether Jewish or non-Jewish, can accomplish the deliverance that all people need. Note also that Paul appeals to an Old-Testament text, from the prophet Habakkuk, to argue that this kind of faith-righteousness, as opposed to self-righteousness, is what God has always required and now has provided.

At the risk of oversimplification, I want to say that if the gospel isn't for Jewish people, the gospel isn't for anyone. If Jewish people don't need the salvation that only Jesus accomplished by his death and resurrection, then nobody needs it. If the gospel fits with any worldview, religion or faith, it especially fits with the one that centers on a personal God who reveals his will through the law and the prophets so that all who believe may be saved, and come to know, worship and enjoy him forever.

We must grasp what Paul could not forget. The arrival of Jesus as promised Messiah resolves a tension that builds throughout the Old Testament. Again and again, a passage will state that God is both holy and loving, righteous and gracious, demanding of holiness and yet ready to forgive. We read our Bibles and ask, *"How this can be?"*. And sooner or later, we must point this out to our Jewish friends. Their Bible creates a problem that only the gospel solves. I'll offer just two examples with the hope that once you see this tension, you'll start to notice it in many other places as well.

First, in that climactic scene on Mount Sinai, the Lord proclaimed:

The LORD, the LORD, the compassionate and gracious God, slow to anger, abounding in love and faithfulness, maintaining love to thousands, and forgiving

> wickedness, rebellion and sin. Yet he does not leave
> the guilty unpunished; he punishes the children and
> their children for the sin of the fathers to the third
> and fourth generation.                    **Exodus 34 v 6-7**

How can the same God be so gracious and yet so demanding? So abounding in lovingkindness and yet so unwilling to leave the guilty unpunished?

Or, to take a poetic example, consider the two sections of Psalm 98. The first three verses call us to sing a new song to the LORD because of his salvation (a term repeated three times in as many verses). God's right hand and his holy arm work salvation because of his lovingkindness and his faithfulness. But the latter part of this psalm (getting twice the airtime as the first part) invites us to shout for joy, burst into jubilant song, make music, and join even the world of nature (sea, rivers, and mountains) in praise. *Why?* Because he judges the world! This is not the happy ending we had been anticipating with all that music.

Again, we ask a vexing question: *How can the same God be so gracious and loving while also being so judging and righteous?* A bit of thoughtful reflection should make us shudder that, if God does indeed judge "with equity," we're all in a heap of trouble. We want to quit reading Exodus 34 before all that punishment stuff and we wouldn't mind leaving off that last verse and a half of Psalm 98 about that equity stuff. And indeed, modern liberal Judaism and much of liberal Protestantism have done exactly that. It may not be as blatant as omitting verses from Scripture readings but the net effect is to emphasize God's love and ignore his holiness.

But what if God eventually resolves the tension his word highlights? What if God demands payment for sin and provides payment for sin? What if he does what we cannot do? He demands atonement but also delivers atonement; he satisfies both his holiness and his grace with one act, showing himself to be both "just and the justifier" (Romans 3 v 26).

The Suffering Servant's atoning death and victorious resurrection (Isaiah 53) display God's love and his holiness. The arrival of the Messiah, told in the Gospels, not only fulfills the predictions, types, and foreshadowings of the Old Testament. It also satisfies the longings of our hearts—we know we should be punished for our sin but hope there's a way of escape that doesn't compromise our demand for justice. The story of Jesus is not some artificial addendum to an otherwise complete story. It is the climax of a story that demands such an ending.

The task of Jewish evangelism involves pointing out the tension in the Old Testament that only finds resolution in the New. It shows the message of Jesus to be a profoundly Jewish message, one that fulfills what needs to be fulfilled—in the text and in our hearts.

Should you deliver such a full-orbed theological dissertation during your first conversation with Jewish friends? Probably not. The second part of this book will address a plan of delivery for this glorious message. At this point, I hope you'll sense the rightness of telling Jewish people about the Jewish Messiah promised by Jewish prophets and anticipated in Jewish history. I plead with you to stand firm in your conviction to tell the good news no matter how resistant your hearers may seem. I pray that

God will use you in ways you might not even believe are possible, so that you will join Paul, that most unlikely Jewish believer in Jesus, who wrote:

Now to him who is able to do immeasurably more than all we ask or imagine, according to his power that is at work within us, to him be glory in the church and in Messiah Jesus throughout all generations, for ever and ever! Amen.

**Ephesians 3 v 20-21**

### Reflection

- What kinds of fears and false perceptions might a Jewish person have about becoming friends with a Christian? How might you start to address some of those concerns?

**Don't** assume that Jewish people know much about the Bible.

**Do** show an interest in what they understand by their Jewishness—Orthodox, Reform, Liberal, etc.—and try to understand what that means for them in their belief and practice. Accept invitations to share in Jewish rituals and festivals

**Don't** underestimate how deeply their misconceptions about Jesus and Christians run.

**Do** be prepared to think differently about how to share the gospel with a Jewish person—they see things in a very different way.

**Don't** rush to demand a response—it can take a long time for Jewish people to understand and appreciate that the gospel is good news for them.

# The different traditions of Judaism

## Orthodox Judaism

This is the most conservative branch of Judaism, adhering most strictly to the teachings of the Hebrew Bible and the traditions of the rabbis. Members of Orthodox synagogues are most likely keep a strict diet (called "kosher") according to the rules in Leviticus, dress with distinctive clothes (long, black coats and wide-brimmed hats) and remain isolated from society. Their worship services are conducted in Hebrew and center on studying the scriptures and applying them strictly and literally to life.

## Reform Judaism

A liberal branch of Judaism, rejecting the need to keep all the observances and laws in the Bible. Reform Jews dress like others in their culture and emphasize cultural and political aspects of Judaism more than religious or spiritual ones. Their worship services are in English and center on learning ethical living and adapting to the world around them. This branch is often called "Liberal Judaism" in the UK and other Commonwealth countries.

## Conservative Judaism

The middle ground between Orthodox and Reform Judaism, keeping many of the traditions but allowing for personal preference in which ones to uphold. Worship services are closer to Orthodox ones but mix Hebrew and English. More Jewish people identify with the Conservative movement than with Orthodox or Reform.

## Reconstructionist Judaism

The most liberal and recent development in Judaism, rejecting literal interpretations of the Bible and emphasizing adaptation to evolving cultures and practices. Some practitioners of Reconstructionist Judaism may not even believe in God but adapt some Jewish practices for cultural, mystical or ceremonial reasons.

These are the main groupings that you are likely to come across. There are some other groupings, such as the Ultra-orthodox or *chasidic (hasidic)* groups, and mystical sects (*Kabbalah*). But as outlined in this chapter, do not assume that if someone attends a particular congregation, they adopt any or all of their beliefs.

# Engaging with Jewish people

# Chapter three

# Prayerful friendship

The most important aspect of evangelism is prayer. That goes without saying. Unfortunately, it often goes without praying.

Reading books on evangelism could lead you to think the process depends on you and you alone. If you just employ the right tactics, remember the best arguments, carry the coolest booklets, and craft the perfect phrases, your witness will bear fruit—or so it could seem. Maybe you have a Jewish friend, and picked up this book because you were looking for a technique that would help convince her about Jesus. Wrong starting point.

Let's not forget that "no one can come to [Jesus] unless the Father ... draws him" (John 6 v 44). As J. I. Packer put it in his landmark book, *Evangelism and the Sovereignty of God*, we are, *"not only to talk to men about God, but also to talk to God about men."*

This all makes perfect sense. But if there's one thing I've learned about prayer it's that it's easy to quit. We lose heart. That's why Jesus told us that parable about the persistent widow who wouldn't quit bothering the judge: so that we would not "give up" (Luke 18 v 1-5). That's why Paul chose the phrase "devote yourselves" to start his admonition to pray and to link prayer to evangelism.

> Devote yourselves to prayer, keeping alert in it with an attitude of thanksgiving; praying at the same time for us as well, that God will open up to us a door for the word, so that we may speak forth the mystery of Christ, for which I have also been imprisoned; that I may make it clear in the way I ought to speak. Conduct yourselves with wisdom toward outsiders, making the most of the opportunity. Let your speech always be with grace, as though seasoned with salt, so that you will know how you should respond to each person.
> **Colossians 4 v 2-6**

We are to "devote ourselves to prayer" because any less of a commitment will run out of steam. And this may be especially the case when it comes to praying for the salvation of Jewish people because, as I've said before, the devil hates them and they have a long history of being resistant to God's leading.

Note that Paul offers two encouragements to help us in our steadfastness. After urging us to devote ourselves to prayer, he adds, **"being watchful and thankful."** We should look for evidence that the great composer is orchestrating events to spark interest and pique curiosity. We should listen for things people say or don't say that might imply a hunger for connection to God. And we should look for opportunities to start conversations that could continue into eternity.

I wonder if I sometimes drag my feet in praying for

God to open hearts of non-believers because I'm afraid he'll answer. Then I'd have to follow his opening doors and opening hearts by opening my mouth! We need to pray for both their hearts and our own.

We're also told to **be thankful.** There's nothing that motivates us to continue to pray quite as much as seeing answers to prayers in the past. I like to keep a journal with dates of when I prayed and when God answered. To be sure, there will be some requests with an empty space in the "answer" column for quite some time. But there will also be plenty of entries with remarkable answers to prayers that should help us to stay vigilant on our knees.

## Establishing and deepening friendships

**Joke:** A young boy once asked his rabbi, *"What are Jews like?"* The rabbi responded, *"Oh, Jews are just like everyone else—only more so!"*

This cute description has a lot of truth to it. And it applies to many areas of life. All people are social creatures. It flows from our "image-of-God-ness" and the fact that our God is a communal, triune God. So we all like to talk and connect and gather. But Jewish people make far more of those interactions than what may be the norm in your cultural background. Jewish people tend to speak of their "congregation" rather than their "synagogue." Note the tilt toward people rather than an institution. Family gatherings are big deals and failure to show up is an even bigger deal.

So you'll want to take steps toward deeper friendships with the Jewish people God places in your neighborhood, at your workplace, or anywhere else you find them. Practically speaking, I urge you to develop three interpersonal skills: asking good questions, listening with empathy, and broaching uncomfortable topics.

## 1. Ask good questions

Why? Funny you should ask! What does a question do that a mere statement doesn't?

Did you see what I did there? I asked you a question and it engaged you in the process of answering far more than if I had just made a statement. (If it didn't engage you in actively wrestling with the issue, I would ask you why!)

Far too many conversations in our fast-paced, smartphone-obsessed world devolve into lower forms of interaction than true dialogue. In fact, "simultaneous monologues" might describe more of our encounters than we'd care to admit. Numerous social scientists bemoan our alienation, loneliness and fragmentedness in today's tech-saturated world. We can buck that trend by deepening friendships with caring conversations that begin with and are laced with thoughtful questions.

Here's another way of thinking about it. If we can't connect well on mundane topics like the weather, how our day is going, what's new, and "lite" topics like that, what are our chances of helping people consider atonement, incarnation, fulfillment of prophecy, forgiveness of sins and eternal life? Better still, when we show people we care about their earthly life by listening well, they may just trust us enough to discuss heavenly topics.

Consider what a professor of Social Studies of Science and Technology at MIT says about conversation:

Face-to-face conversation is the most human—and humanizing—thing we do. Fully present to one another, we learn to listen. It's where we develop the capacity for empathy. It's where we experience the joy of being heard, of being understood. And conversation advances self-reflection, the conversations with ourselves that are the cornerstone of early development and continue throughout life.[1]

Here are some suggestions for becoming a good questioner:

- **Develop a short list of questions you feel comfortable asking at the beginning of a relationship.** (e.g. Where are you from? What do you like to do with your free time? What kind of work are you involved in?)
- **Develop another list of questions that take things a bit deeper.** (e.g. What are some of your favorite movies? Books? Authors? Where would you like to go for an ideal vacation?)
- **Resist the temptation to just start talking about yourself when they stop talking about themselves.** Ask a follow-up question to probe further.
- **Consider answering a question with a question instead of an answer.** It's a very Jewish thing to do. (e.g. They ask, *"Don't you think all religions are basically the same?"* You could ask, *"Do you think so? How did you come to that conclusion?"*)

---

1  Sherry Turkle, *Reclaiming Conversation: The Power of Talk in a Digital Age,* London, Penguin (2015), page 3.

- **Limit your use of "why" questions.** They can come across as attacking. *"Why did you wear that shirt today"* can sound like a critique or an expression of dislike.
- **Prepare a short list of questions you could ask to shift a conversation toward spiritual topics.** e.g. Do you ever think much about spiritual things? What part has faith played in your life? I know you've told me you're Jewish. Would you ever be interested in telling me more about your faith? I'd be very interested.

## 2. Listen with empathy

It's one thing to gather information—a rather important thing. Knowing (and remembering!) where they're from, how many kids they have, what they do for a living, and other "data" helps you find common ground and deepen a friendship. But it's also good to listen "between the lines," to notice tone of voice, to catch facial expressions, to hear what's behind the words. At some point (and we must be careful not to jump to this too soon in a relationship or conversation) we might express an observation about how they just said what they just said. It could sound like this:

- *"You sound excited about that! Could you tell me more?"*
- *"I sense there's more to that. Am I right?"*
- *"Oooh. I think I just struck a nerve. Should I change the subject?"*
- *"You don't sound too happy about that. I'd be willing to listen some more, if you'd like to talk about that."*

Choosing to keep the conversational spotlight on them, instead of constantly hijacking the conversation to focus on yourself, could express a kind of respect, concern or care for your Jewish friend that could pave the way for deeper friendship and, hopefully, willingness to explore deeper topics.

### 3. Be willing to bring up difficult topics

For the vast majority of conversations with Jewish people, Jesus won't just "come up". He's a forbidden, painful and unexplored subject for discussion. If you wait until it seems smooth or easy or natural, you'll probably be waiting forever. You may need to confess (as I often do) that I value comfort far more than I should. In fact, there are times I *worship* comfort. Such idolatry fails to acknowledge God's pre-eminence or seek his glory. So there are times that I pray two simultaneous prayers as I open my mouth—"*God, please set me free from the idolatry of comfort and set them free to receive the good news.*"

You may need to begin bringing up unwanted topics by having "a conversation about the conversation." In other words, it might be wise to acknowledge the elephant in the room: that such topics are often neglected or avoided. Or you may need to ask permission to venture into areas that most people avoid at all costs. You may need to say something like this:

> We've talked about a lot of things, and I really value our friendship. I wonder if you'd be willing to talk about religious things. They're pretty important to me. I know most people stay away from such things. But I think our friendship can handle it. What do you think?

Having "a conversation about the conversation" can also remove a barrier that has limited deep conversation for many people for many years. Your attempt to do so could sound like this:

> I know people say you should never broach contro- versial topics like religion and politics. But I wonder why. Can't we delve into deep things like faith and beliefs without getting angry or insulting? I know a lot of people say we should keep these things private but, if they're really so important, shouldn't they be discussed?

This may not go well. But it's worth trying. Silence about Jesus is never "golden."

A "conversation about the conversation" may also need to address the issue of conversion. Christians see efforts to persuade people to believe in Jesus as central to their faith. Jewish people see it as anathema. This is tricky and needs to be confronted sooner or later. Don't be surprised if your Jewish friend blurts out, *"Are you try-ing to convert me?"* or *"I think it's disgusting that anyone would try to convert someone to their way of thinking."* You'll want to think through this issue carefully for yourself and then plan what you might actually say. Don't neglect this preparation, hoping you'll be brilliant on the spot.

Regarding how you think about conversion, it's crucial to see that **everyone** tries to convert people to their way of thinking. It's unavoidable. Your Jewish friend's state-ment that *"no one should try to convert others to their way of thinking"* is his effort to convert you to *his* way of thinking.

You want to convert him to believe in Jesus as the Messiah, and he wants to convert you to a form of Christianity that doesn't try to convert people to believe in Jesus as the Messiah. You're both trying to convert each other.

How you go about saying this may take some work—and some repetition. The "no one should ever try to convert anyone" stance is a firmly-held, sacred cow in our "tolerant" age, and Jewish people have long benefitted from people leaving them alone about their faith. Entire Christian denominations have issued statements that Jewish people no longer need to be objects of missionary activities. Your Jewish friends will wonder why you haven't arrived at the same level of enlightenment that their liberal Protestant or Catholic acquaintances have. But don't buckle under. Realize that *they* want to convert *you* to this form of non-evangelizing Christianity that finds absolutely no support in the Bible.

Depending on your level of closeness to your Jewish friend, you might respond in one of the following ways to their accusation: *"Are you trying to convert me?"*

- **Option 1—the bold response:** *"Of course I am! What kind of a Christian would I be if I didn't want to convert you?"*
- **Option 2—the nuanced response:** *"Convert? That's a pretty loaded word. I do want to discuss how a Jewish person could believe in Jesus as the Jewish Messiah. It's not such an odd concept as you might think."*
- **Option 3—the turn-the-tables response:** *"But aren't you trying to convert me right now? Don't you want me to change my beliefs from the kind of faith that tries to*

*convert others? C'mon, let's be honest. We're both trying to convert each other."*

- **Option 4—the direct response:** *"Yes. I am trying to convert you. Believing in Jesus has been the most wonderful thing in my life. And it's a very Jewish thing. I can't think of anything more I would want for you than for you to find what I've found."*

You'll need to pay attention to a tricky balance of two factors when talking to Jewish people about Jesus.

**First, Christianity is *very* Jewish.** The New Testament was written by Jewish people, initially for a predominately Jewish audience, trying to sort out how Jesus' words and actions fitted with the Jewish scriptures that came before him. In your mind, the Jewishness of Jesus seems undeniable, obvious and central. But to most Jewish people, this is far from obvious. In fact, it's the exact opposite. Everything about Christianity seems alien, bizarre, hostile, and about as *"goyish"* (i.e. Gentile in the least attractive way) as possible. Thus, you'll want to bring up things that seem obvious to you but will seem odd to them.

**Second, your "love" for the Jewish people might not be received as such.** Some Gentile Christians gush a bit too much for Jewish people to feel comfortable around them. *"Oh, I just love the Jews,"* I've heard some well-meaning Christians say. Most of my relatives would either roll their eyes or turn and run. Effusive expressions of love for the Jewish people sound suspect in Jewish ears. Yes, you should express your appreciation of, and concern for, the state of Israel, the wellbeing of Jewish people in a world of rising anti-Semitism, etc. But understatement will go farther than overstatement.

Having said this, I want to issue a caution. Some Gentile Christians are a bit naïve about their positive views of Jewish people. They see Jewish people as holier than they really are. On the surface some Orthodox Jewish people appear pious, devout and prayerful. They remain steadfast in their worship of God even though they've endured such evil at the hands of those who want to wipe them off the face of the earth. So, naïvely and unbiblically, some Christians attribute a level of holiness to Jewish people that the Scriptures preclude. Remember, it's not just a New Testament concept that "all have sinned and fall short of the glory of God" (see Romans 3 v 23). The writer of Ecclesiastes boldly and universally proclaimed, "There is no one on earth who is righteous, no one who does what is right and never sins" (Ecclesiastes 7 v 20).

Related to this naïveté, some Christians have supported Jewish relief agencies in Israel that claim to merely offer food, shelter, and language training for Jewish immigrants moving from foreign lands. Rabbi Yechiel Eckstein has raised quite a bit of money from naïve Christians who fail to see that he has an anti-missionary agenda woven into his "humanitarian" efforts. Eckstein may have changed his tone but not his convictions from when he wrote, "*Any deliberate attempt to convert Jews to Christianity can be seen only as a more subtle form of Hitler's 'final solution'—the plan to erase Jews from the face of the earth.*"[1] Far better to donate

---

1 Yechiel Eckstein, *What Christians Should Know About Jews and Judaism*, Word (1984), page 293.

your funds to a gospel-centered ministry that shares the good news while doing good deeds.

I have one final thought before moving on. Don't let my cautions scare you away from introducing Jesus and proclaiming the good news of his messiah-ship. God's word is powerful and his truth is self-authenticating. Sometimes the simplest, clearest, most non-nuanced statements of the gospel penetrate in unpredictable ways. Start, even if you don't know where it will go. Begin conversations even if you feel timid. Testify to what you know, and then trust God to provide words for what you don't yet know. Ask God to take your feeble efforts and use them in ways only he can. Watch God work in tandem with your less-than-perfect, far-from-polished ways. God's word is a two-edged sword. Don't keep it tucked safely in a sheath.

**Reflection**

- Are you truly *devoted* to praying for your friends, family, neighbours and colleagues who do not know Jesus? How can you help yourself to be more consistent in pleading with the Lord for those who are lost without Christ?

- How are you building *real* friendships with your Jewish friends? Are you listening, sharing, and talking about life in a way which will make talking about spiritual things more welcome?

- If you have a Jewish friend, how might you have a "conversation about the conversation"? Decide how to broach the subject, and pray for courage to do it.

# Dan's story

By the age of 18, Dan's life had spiraled down to the point where he was contemplating suicide every day. His parents' divorce and other "family implosions" drove him to escape through the diversions of dating, band gigs, and dabbling in the occult. His Jewish upbringing—along with a love for literature, including Greek mythology—gave way to playing in rock bands, broken relationships and hanging out with a bad crowd, leading to despair and hopelessness.

To this emotional flight, he added intellectual and spiritual exploration. He said, *"If the other religions like Christianity, Buddhism, Islam and Hinduism are just like Greek mythology, then they're lies and idolatry."* The only option left to him was the occult, which fitted well with the heavy metal scene. He felt so much pain and saw so little hope that he made a conscious decision to kill himself. After a long walk around his neighborhood, he turned toward his house, where he determined he'd end his torment.

As he approached his house around 10pm, he saw his friend Jill standing in his driveway. Their conversation began like this:

Dan: *"Jill, I need to say goodbye"*

Jill: *"But I just got here."*

Dan: *"No. You don't understand. I mean 'Goodbye. For the last time.'"*

Jill: *"What do you mean?"*

Dan: *"I've decided life's too hard and too painful. I can't take it anymore. I'm going to kill myself. I have nothing to live for."*

Jill: *"Well, can I tell you what I live for?"*

Dan really didn't want to hear what she had to say but

felt it would be too rude to say, *"No. I'd rather be dead than hear what you believe about Jesus."* Besides, he reasoned, *"She believes lies and lies can't hurt me. So I'll listen. It won't make any difference."*

She spoke about her faith in Jesus and how it gave her hope. Today, Dan says, *"I can't recount a lot of content from that conversation. I don't remember many of the details. She explained things and, in my mind, it was like fireworks on the fourth of July. And she was talking about things about my God, the God of Abraham, Isaac and Jacob, the God of the Bible. She knew things about that God that I didn't know."*

What stood out was that Jill talked about this God as if she really knew him—personally. *"I knew about God, that he parted the Red Sea and all that. I believed that actually happened. That wasn't like those Greek myths. But I didn't know that you could actually know this God. When God gave that name, "I am that I am," that wasn't even an actual name. And as Jews, we weren't even allowed to ever say that word out loud. We couldn't even write it! So he wasn't any kind of God that you could get to know in a personal way ... the way Jill was talking about him."*

He asked questions and she responded patiently—for over five hours! Finally, he grew tired and needed some sleep. So he said, *"Jill, I'm too tired to even think straight any more. But I promise you: I won't kill myself until we speak again. I want to talk more about this."* And they did. A lot. Less than 48 hours after that five-hour conversation, Dan knew: *"Jesus was the Messiah. He could save me. He wanted to save me. And he was the only one who could save me and protect me from evil"*—the evil that had engulfed his life up until that point in time. *"He saved me and made me a new creation."*

# Chapter four

# Pointing to the Scriptures

Sooner or later (and the sooner, the better) you'll want to urge your Jewish friends to read the Bible for themselves. In particular, you'll want them to read the gospel according to Matthew, a very Jewish approach to telling the story of Jesus.

You want them to see in print what Jesus said about himself and how his teachings fit with the history of Israel and the words of the prophets. Let them encounter how brilliant, how unpredictable, how gracious, how bold, and how beautiful Jesus was and is. Pray that they'll see the wide gulf between what they thought they'd find and what they actually do find. Ask God to open their eyes to see the truth they never allowed themselves to see, and to feel the wonder of meeting the Messiah they've only heard about in vague platitudes.

You'll need to decide beforehand what terms you'll use to talk about the Bible. I would simply refer to what is sometimes called "the Old Testament" as "the Bible." You could call it "the Scriptures" but that may not connect with some Jewish people. I would avoid the term "Old Testament" completely and not resort to calling it "the older testament," even though that does have some nice qualities about it. I would not use the term *"Tanach"* (a Hebrew acrostic referring to the three parts of the Bible: the Law, the Prophets and the Writings) because Jewish people may not know that term or they may think you're trying too hard to sound as if you know Hebrew when you really don't.

One friend of mine, with years of experience in Jewish evangelism, gave me this advice:

> I sometimes like calling the Old Testament the *Hebrew Bible*. If I'm giving a Jewish person a Bible, I might say, "This Bible has both the Hebrew Scriptures and the New Testament in it. Christians often refer to the Hebrew Scriptures as the Old Testament, but they still believe that those Scriptures are very important and relevant even though they call it old." If they want to know why we call it "Old" and the New "New", then I'll explain.

I think it's fine to use the term "New Testament" but you might have to explain that you realize this is "a part of the Bible most Jewish people don't accept." Acknowledge that elephant in the room and try to save the apologetics about why the New Testament is the inspired word of God for later. You've already ventured into the awkward waters of encouraging them to read about Jesus. Admit that this may feel different but then point them back to the subject at hand.

They may want to use a copy of the Bible they received when they were young. That's great. But you should b eprepared for a translation that might seem a bit antiquated, and you'll want to remember that the order of the books in their Bible differs a bit from yours. Don't make a big deal about this. All the books are there. The table of contents will help you both find what you're looking for.

If they don't own their own copy of the Bible, be careful about providing one too casually. If they're not ready to read the Bible, just giving them one might make them feel uncomfortable. Your gift might just collect dust on their shelf (probably a hidden shelf where Jewish relatives won't see it). It might be wiser to lend them a copy of the Bible and/or a New Testament and see how they respond. If they buy their own copy, that may be best of all. You could start by inviting them to read Matthew and discuss it with you. Use Matthew's references to the Old Testament as a way to affirm how the "two parts of the Bible" fit together.

Focus on showing what the Bible says about the three major topics mentioned earlier—God, people and eternity. Their Bible and the New Testament agree wholeheartedly about all three. But you may have to demonstrate that some of their strongly held convictions about God or people or eternity don't line up with the Bible as much as they assume.

## 1. God

Highlight your agreement with Judaism's emphasis on the holiness of God. Affirm that God created the world, sustains it, gave commandments for people to live by—commandments that, if obeyed, will lead to a life of flourishing—and wants people to know, worship and obey him. Become fluent in quoting Scriptures that declare God's holiness (e.g. Isaiah 6 v 3), his love (e.g. Jeremiah 31 v 3), and the fact that we can know him (e.g. Psalm 16 v 11).

But, you may ask, what about the Christian belief in the Trinity? Isn't that a huge obstacle to overcome? Yes, but not yet. Early on, focus on Jesus and his many, many, many claims to be more than a mere man. Allow that component of our belief in the Trinity (Jesus' deity) to settle in before hefty theological lectures about "three-in-oneness." In fact, for some Jewish people, once they accept Jesus' claims to be God (no easy task!), acceptance of the doctrine of the Trinity seems to follow without much fanfare.

We'll examine this more in depth in the chapter on answering objections. You can minimize the enormity of this objection by asking questions like, *"Aren't there some things about God that we will never fully comprehend?"* or *"If God is who he says he is and we're merely human, wouldn't it make sense that some things about him would be beyond our ability to understand?"*

## 2. People

You'll need to show that we're not as good as most Jewish people think. To be sure, we're created in God's image

(Genesis 1 v 26-27), granted great dignity (Psalm 8 v 4-5), and called to pursue justice in the world (Micah 6 v 8). But we're also terribly sinful. You'll need to show them these things in their copy of the Bible (so they don't think this is some Christian distortion of the Bible) that we're all in a lot of trouble. The prophets taught it.

> The heart is deceitful above all things and beyond cure.
>                                                    **Jeremiah 17 v 9**

> Surely the arm of the LORD is not too short to save, nor his ear too dull to hear. But your iniquities have separated you from your God; your sins have hidden his face from you, so that he will not hear.
>                                                    **Isaiah 59 v 1-2**

And numerous prophets spoke of Israel's turning away from God as nothing less than disgusting adultery. Ezekiel's lengthy allegory (all of his sixteenth chapter) might be a good homework reading assignment for them (and you!). Do all that you can so they feel the weight of the Scriptures' condemnation of sin. Only then will they appreciate how wonderful God's salvation can be.

Speaking of salvation, you'll want them to see that it's a big deal in their Bible even if it has faded into the background of modern Jewish thought. Consult a concordance to see how often the word "salvation" appears in the prophets and the psalms, and let them wonder why their rabbi hardly ever mentions the idea. The final stanza of one of the most beautiful and well-known Hebrew prayers, *Avinu Malkeinu,* recited every year on *Rosh*

*Hashanah*, one of the "high holidays," brings this truth to the surface in profound ways:

> Our Father, Our King, be Thou gracious unto us and answer us, for lo, we are unworthy [literally—we have no good works of our own]; deal Thou with us in charity and loving-kindness and save us.[1]

## 3. Eternity

When addressing what the Scriptures teach about eternity, it is best to move gradually away from the common Jewish view that *"we don't really think about life after death too much"* to the Christian view of *"What good will it be for a man if he gains the whole world, yet forfeits his soul?"* You might want to try some intermediate steps such as:

- *"Well, if God is eternal, wouldn't it make sense that he'd want us to think about eternity?"*
- *"Isn't it possible for us to have more certainty than just, 'we'll find out when we get there'?"*
- *"I think God has given us more insight into eternity than we usually realize."*

Our message when considering eternity or life after death must include three crucial components: **the person of Jesus, the importance of the resurrection**, and **the fulfillment of prophecy**—not necessarily in that order. Wouldn't it be nice if all paths to conversion followed the same sequence?

---

1 Morris Silverman, ed. *High Holiday Prayer Book*, New York, Prayer Book Press (1951), page 96.

For some people, the starting point is messianic prophecy. For others, it's meeting Jesus in the Gospels. For others, it's squaring the teachings of the New and Old Testaments. As with the rest of humankind, we dare not insist on a "one size fits all" approach to Jewish evangelism. The common denominator, however, should be the centrality of the Scriptures. If they do indeed "testify of" Jesus, let's allow the two-edged sword to work.

I have already written of my experience of meeting Jesus in my reading of the New Testament and finding him to be so very different than I expected him to be. I was told he was just a good rabbi. But I could not see how such a mundane description could apply to a man who claimed to be the Messiah (John 4 v 25-26), God himself (John 8 v 58), one who could forgive sins (Mark 2 v 5-7), one who always existed and will continue to exist for all time (Matthew 28 v 20), and the only way to God (John 14 v 6). Introduce your Jewish friends to this Jesus through the pages of the Gospels and allow them to wrestle with the incongruity between the Jesus they meet there and the Jesus they've been told about. Pray that God will use this truth to cut through the false images and open their eyes. And be kind to them along the way. It hurts when you realize your rabbi, your parents, the vast majority of your people, and the dominant relativistic spirit of our age have all been wrong.

Pray that they'll arrive at the kind of clarity of thought expressed by C. S. Lewis here in his essay "What are we to make of Jesus Christ?"

There is no halfway house and there is no parallel

in other religions. If you had gone to Buddha and asked him, "Are you the son of Bramah?" he would have said, "My son, you are still in the vale of illusion." If you had gone to Socrates and asked, "Are you Zeus?" he would have laughed at you. If you had gone to Mohammed and asked, "Are you Allah?" he would first have rent his clothes and then cut your head off. If you had asked Confucius, "Are you Heaven?", I think he would have probably replied, "Remarks which are not in accordance with nature are in bad taste." The idea of a great moral teacher saying what Christ said is out of the question. In my opinion, the only person who can say that sort of thing is either God or a complete lunatic suffering from that form of delusion which undermines the whole mind of man.[1]

The reality of the resurrection is the climax of the story of Jesus. And so it should take center stage in our presentations of the gospel. Somehow, for many Christians, the fact that Jesus rose from the dead has slipped into the background behind his teaching or other aspects of the Christian life. But if Jesus did not rise from the dead, as Paul so powerfully declared, our *"faith is futile; [we] are still in our sins..."* and *"we are to be pitied more than all men"* (1 Cor 15 v 17-19). I wouldn't necessarily lead with a discussion of the resurrection but, at some point, we must declare this truth in a way that transfers all prior discussion from the realms of opinion, theory or philoso-

---

1 C. S. Lewis, *God in the Dock*, Eerdmans (1970), pages 157-158.

phy and brings it into the arena of history, fact and a settled reality. The fact of the resurrection changes the way we think about everything else Jesus said and did, and how we understand all of the Bible. It is that monumental, and our Jewish friends need to feel the enormity of its weight. It is not hard to find ample evidence and arguments in support for the resurrection. Do a little bit of homework to prepare yourself for this essential task of Christian apologetics.

## Messianic prophecy

And now we arrive at the discussion of the wonder-filled topic of messianic prophecy. In a book of this size and scope, I can only begin to scratch the surface. I have heard several people compare the Bible to the ocean. Young children can wade into it up to just their ankles and it can provide hours of pleasure and wonder. Or teams of oceanographers can spend their entire lives plunging as far as possible in sophisticated submarines with the best of research equipment, and still not fathom all that is there. So it is with the rich, complex, beautiful, and inexhaustible topic of fulfillment of prophecy.

As we wade in, we can marvel at just a mere listing of ways in which the Messiah was prophesied in various parts of the Bible, and how Jesus fulfilled those Scriptures. Consider the following brief list:

- **The Messiah as a person, born of a woman:** Genesis 3 v 15 / Matthew 1 v 18 - 25
- **Messiah's birthplace:** Micah 5 v 2 / Matthew 2 v 1
- **Messiah's birth from a virgin:** Isaiah 7 v 14 / Matthew 1 v 18-23

- **The forerunner of the Messiah:** Isaiah 40 v 3-5 / Matthew 3 v 1-3; Malachi 3 v 1 / Matthew 11 v 10, Mark 1 v 2, Luke 1 v 76, 7 v 27; Malachi 4 v 5 / Matthew 11 v 14, 17 v 10-12, Mark 9 v 11-13, Luke 1 v 16-17
- **The suffering of the Messiah:** Psalm 22 v 7 / Matthew 27 v 39, Mark 15 v 29, Luke 23 v 35; Psalm 22 v 8 / Matthew 27 v 43; Zechariah 12 v 10 / John 19 v 37; Isaiah 52 v 13 – 53 v 12 / 1 Peter 2 v 21-25 / Acts 8 v 32-35
- **The resurrection of the Messiah:** Psalm 16 v 10

And this is just a tiny subset of literally hundreds of connections between the Old and New Testaments.[1]

For many Jewish people, discussion of prophecy at this level suffices. But you should be prepared if your Jewish friend wants a ride in a submarine to dive deeper. And for your own growth as a student of the Scriptures, I hope you'll dig in and see just how the prophets wrote about the Anointed One, how the history of Israel foreshadows the Redeemer, and how shadowy images find their clearest display in the Lion of the tribe of Judah.

If you could survey the entire Hebrew Bible and highlight all the prophecies of the Messiah, you would first note there are a lot of them—over 800 according to some scholars. You would also note that some are rather direct and others are indirect or downright puzzling. You would also see that the vast majority (some have estimated about 500 of the 800) speak of a time of peace

---

1 A fuller list can be found in an appendix to Moishe Rosen's book *Witnessing to Jews* Purple Pomegranate Productions (1998), pages 201-203. It's a pretty lengthy list.

and total reversal of the curses of Genesis 3. Images of wolves and lambs feeding together (Isaiah 65 v 25) and people beating their swords into plowshares (Isaiah 2 v 4) paint serene pictures of a time drastically different than the world in which we now live. That's why so many Jewish people reject out of hand the notion that the Messiah has already arrived. They might ask, with not a slight amount of sarcasm, *"Have you read the newspaper lately? What makes you think the Messiah has already come?"*

Far too many well-meaning Gentile Christians have concluded that Jewish people must be stupid or blind not to see that Jesus fulfills Old Testament prophecy. But the questioning of eyesight goes in both directions. Jewish people think Christians are equally clueless for not seeing all the suffering in the world that the coming of the Messiah was supposed to eradicate.

The problem stems from the fact that the Scriptures paint two different portraits of the Messiah: one a conquering king who inaugurates a time of peace (e.g. Zechariah 14 v 9-11) and another who suffers an atoning death (e.g. Isaiah 53). A few diligent rabbis who took all the data into account wondered if perhaps God might send two Messiahs—a "Messiah, son of David" who would reign on a throne and a "Messiah, son of Joseph," who would suffer unjustly at the hands of evil people (similar to the way Joseph suffered at the hands of his brothers).

This "two Messiahs" theory isn't bad. We should affirm that it takes into account both kinds of messianic predictions. We, however, think it's best to see only one Messiah who comes twice. That's why Zechariah predicted that when Messiah comes:

> They will look on me, the one they have pierced,
> and they will mourn for him as one mourns for an
> only child, and grieve bitterly for him as one grieves
> for a firstborn son. **Zechariah 12 v 10**

He came the first time and was "pierced." He will come a second time and will reign.

With this as a brief introduction to the complex world of prophecy, keep in mind these three points that will particular help in Jewish evangelism.

**First, the New Testament writers, and the Christian interpreters who followed them, identified the same passages as messianic that Jewish rabbis have done for centuries.** Christians did not distort the Old Testament or see things that weren't really there. Alfred Edersheim, a biblical scholar in the 19th century, documents in *The Life and Times of Jesus the Messiah* an impressive list of over 450 references to ancient rabbinic authors who attributed Old Testament Scriptures to the Messiah.[1] They chose the same passages that Matthew, Paul, and Peter selected, using similar methods of biblical interpretation.

**Second, there are good reasons why these passages should be interpreted as messianic.** But it's not quite as simple as you might think. A quick, cursory reading of some parts of the Bible (why would you want to read such an important book in such a shallow way?) might make you wonder why anyone would think there's a Messiah lurking in there. But numerous clues suggest more going

---

1 Alfred Edersheim, *The Life and Times of Jesus the Messiah*, Grand Rapids, Eerdemans (1971), pages 710-741.

on than the immediate context of the narrative.

For example, some texts contain odd terms or phrases that slow readers down and spark curiosity. Genesis 3 v 15 (a text Jewish scholars have long believed as referring to the Messiah) says the *"seed of the woman"* will *"crush the head"* of the seed of the serpent. Isn't that odd? Readers who were moving along well through this chapter, finding no difficulty interpreting the curses meted out to the woman and the man, suddenly come to this head-and-heel-crushing couplet and scratch their heads. The very oddness of the promise deliberately intrigues so as to slow the reader down, almost the same way those rumble strips slow drivers down as they approach tollbooths.

In other places, the biblical text points beyond the immediate setting by spending too much time or using loftier language than the current situation would warrant. In fact, some passages seem like bizarre exaggerations. For example, in Psalm 22, David complains that his dire circumstances make him cry out, "My God, my God, why hast thou forsaken me?" And he doesn't quit there. He adds, "All my bones are out of joint" and "they divide my garments among them and cast lots for my clothing" (verses 1, 17, 18).

Either David is exaggerating narcissistically or he's prophesying gloriously. Several rabbinic interpreters thought these statements had to find fulfillment in someone other than David. The Gospel writers, under the inspiration of the Holy Spirit, agreed.

**Third, the prophets wore bifocals.** This makes reading the prophets particularly challenging. They spoke words of warning, encouragement or condemnation to their immediate setting. But they also saw those events or circumstances as foreshadowings of future events. For example, Hosea saw Israel's slavery in Egypt as a foreshadowing of impending attacks by the Assyrians (see Hosea 7 v 11, 16; 8 v 13; 9 v 3, 6; 11 v 5). His coupling of Egypt and Assyria in poetic parallelism added emotional punch to his warnings, while pointing to the God who works similarly in all periods of time.

To add a degree of difficulty, the prophets saw events in the future with such clarity and confidence that they sometimes spoke of future events as having *already happened*. Scholars sometimes call this "the prophetic past tense." It could make you dizzy if you don't remember this.

Perhaps the most complex (and controversial) example comes from Isaiah 7. King Ahaz feared attacks from enemies in the north. Isaiah prophesied a word of comfort that the king had nothing to worry about as long as he trusted in the LORD. And, despite Ahaz's false humility ("I will not ask; I will not put the LORD to the test"—7 v 12), Isaiah offers one sign with both immediate relevance and long-term prediction. God would send a child who would provide visual evidence of God's salvation from their enemies. In the short term, that child appeared in the next chapter of Isaiah. And his presence coincided with God's deliverance of Ahaz and Israel.

But Isaiah looked through the other lens of his bifocals and kept talking about the child for a long time (three more chapters!) and with exalted language—"Wonderful Counselor, Mighty God, Everlasting Father, Prince of Peace" (Isaiah 9 v 6). I'm sure the child born in chapter 8 was a delight to his parents but no mere mortal could live up to the language of chapter 9. So who was the prophecy in chapter 7 about? *The Messiah of course!* But God provided a down payment of the fulfillment of that prophecy through the child born in chapter 8. In similar ways, who was David talking about in Psalm 22? *The Messiah of course!* But God provided David's experiences as down payments of that greater Sufferer yet to come.

## Isaiah 53

Another powerful example of this foreshadow-fulfillment motif, and the most important prophecy that you must discuss with your Jewish friends, is Isaiah 53. (It actually begins at 52 v 13). Some Christians have just read this passage aloud without telling their Jewish friend where it was from. When they asked their friend to guess its source, the inevitable response was *"From the Christian part of the Bible."* Then the wise Gentile believer would reveal that *"it's actually from the Jewish part."* Again, for many Jewish people, this level of study is sufficient. They're now ready to hear how Jesus fulfilled Isaiah 53 by reading the Gospels.

But for those who want to dig in and find out who "the servant" is in this passage, you'll want to prepare yourself for that level of investigation. Isaiah identifies the servant as Israel when we first hear of him in chapter 41. In chapter 42, the servant is not identified at all, raising our curiosity, especially when we read that the servant "establishes justice on the earth" (v 44). Isaiah again identifies the servant as Israel in chapters 44, 45, 48, and 49 v 3.

But he rules out the possibility of equating the servant with Israel in 49 v 5 by saying the servant will "bring Jacob back to [the LORD] and gather Israel to himself." The servant can't be Israel, because he's working on behalf of Israel! Israel, the servant, (the one in Isaiah 41, 44, 45, 48, and 49 v 3) is a down payment and points to a greater Servant, a "servant par excellence" yet to come (the one in Isaiah 52 v 13 – 53 v 12).

You and your Jewish friend may wonder why God inspired such a confusing series of prophecies. Don't wander down that distracting rabbit trail for too long. Suffice it to say, these patterns of down payment and fulfillment build curiosity, anticipation and longing in powerful ways.

This song is the longest, most poetic, and therefore climactic celebration of the servant's work, and it exalts him for his atonement for all who, like sheep, have gone astray. No wonder the early rabbis attributed this beautiful poem as referring to no one other than the Messiah.

Should you share this complex interpretation with all Jewish people? Certainly not. But when some of them charge you and the New Testament writers with playing fast and loose with the text, it's best to prepare yourself to show them that your interpretation (and Matthew's and Paul's, etc.) makes sense, squares with the prophetic way of thinking, and finds support from many influential rabbis across the ages. Better yet, these passages point them to the One who "was pierced for our transgressions" and "crushed for our iniquities."

## The message we must convey

I realize this discussion of Messianic prophecy may overwhelm you. Worse, it might discourage you from ever taking first steps toward presenting the gospel to your

Jewish friends. I hope you won't allow that to happen. The power of evangelism comes from God's word and his Spirit, not our brilliance. Do not underestimate the ways God could use a simple presentation of what you know to be true from the Scriptures. It could sound as succinct and as clear as this:

- **First, we know that God is both holy and loving, as the Scriptures proclaim.** Isaiah said, "Holy, holy, holy is the LORD Almighty; the whole earth is full of his glory" (Isaiah 6 v 3).

- **Second, we know we were created in God's image but we've damaged that image through our sin.** As the book of Ecclesiastes says, "there is no one on earth who is righteous, no one who does what is right and never sins." (Ecclesiastes 7 v 20).

- **Third, we know God promised a Messiah who would atone for our sins and, ultimately, make all things right.** Numerous prophets foretold his arrival and gave him wonderful titles. In one place he's called the "servant" who would be "pierced for our transgressions" (Isaiah 53 v 5).

- **Finally, we all need to respond to God's works by acknowledging our need and accepting God's provision.** Consider this gracious invitation from God, recorded by Isaiah: "Come, all you who are thirsty, come to the waters; and you who have no money, come, buy and eat!...Give ear and come to me; hear me, that your soul may live" (Isaiah 55 v 1, 3).

# Sally's story

Sally's life revolved around her boyfriend and her band. From the time she was young, she wanted to write music and perform. And, before reaching 20 years old, she had a great start toward both those goals, landing a job at a recording studio, singing in a band, and being offered a recording contract. She had moved from California to London to be close to the British rock scene and started making connections for a fast track to fame.

Her boyfriend was another story. He treated her poorly, disrespected her, and demanded obedience in ways that Sally could never fulfill. She dulled the pain through the party lifestyle that came with the music. But, after losing her visa and needing to move back to America, her band fired her and her boyfriend dumped her. The two most important things in her life were gone. She remembers that time like this: *"I was a complete mess and seriously needed help."*

So she started to look to religion for answers. *"I thought I could probably find the answers to life's biggest and most difficult questions in my religion. I was Jewish. Why shouldn't I find answers in Judaism?"* She took several books about Judaism out from the library and also had conversations with her brother. His answers revolved around Jesus so she dismissed them out of hand. *"The only thing I really understood about being Jewish was that Jews didn't believe in Jesus ... and I wanted nothing to do with Jesus,"* she recalls.

But the books about Judaism didn't help. They told her that, if she wanted to be happy, she needed to choose to obey God by observing his laws. *"All I could think was that I had already been in a relationship with a guy I could never seem to please, so why would I want to en-*

ter into a relationship with a God who is just going to make more demands on my life? Disillusioned, I closed the books, but the questions wouldn't go away."

One late night after an evening of heavy partying, feeling sad and empty, she began to read the New Testament her brother had given her. "I started reading Matthew, the first book of the New Testament. What I read stunned me. It was the genealogy of Jesus. Jesus was a Jew! I knew this to be true, but I had never given it much thought. But there it was in front of me: he was related to Abraham, Isaac, and Jacob, King David and Solomon, and the list went on. I began to question: 'Okay, if he's Jewish, maybe it's okay for me to read this ... and maybe even trust it.' I kept reading.

"What I began to notice was that Jesus gathered people around him regardless of their ethnicity, their position in life, or their religious background. He met with people where they were. The people he would talk to didn't have to be religious Jews, those who observed the Torah unswervingly. No, he spoke to the 'sinners', the rejects of the world, the broken people, because they had a hunger to know the truth. They needed healing, and they needed hope. They needed to be loved in spite of their circumstances. That was me.

"I began crying, and I couldn't stop. At once, I was filled with joy and sorrow: joy that I felt a freedom I had never experienced before, and sorrow that I had refused to accept the truth about Jesus for so long. I wept over my years of seeking love and approval from others instead of resting in the love, acceptance, and salvation of my Creator provided though Jesus. I wept over seeking my own glory, instead of the glory of the one true God."

**Reflection**

- Are you confident that you could share the gospel at a simple, outline level to a friend who asked, *"What is the message of Christianity?"* How might you train yourself if you are not confident to do that?

- Do you have a proper grasp of the character of God, the glory and sinfulness of humanity, and the Christian hope for eternity? What key Scriptures might you point to if you get the opportunity to explain to someone?

- How familiar are you with the Old Testament? Would you be able to hold an intelligent discussion on the details of the Hebrew Scriptures with someone who knew them well?

- Continue to pray for opportunities to share the good news with a Jewish friend.

# Chapter five

# Answering objections

B y now, you may realize you should assume a certain level of resistance to the good news from Jewish people. Your gospel presentation or preliminary conversations about Jesus may get some pushback. Your attitude toward them can either pave the way toward belief or add thickness to already constructed walls. Jude's admonition to "be merciful to those who doubt" (v 22) applies to those outside the household of faith as well as strugglers within. Ask God for kindness in tone of voice as well as clarity in expression of words.

All Christians should constantly add to their evangelistic toolboxes by searching out books, articles, websites, and other resources that answer non-Christians' questions from a variety of perspectives and with a variety of depth. Some books (like Tim Keller's *The Reason for God* or C. S. Lewis's *Mere Christianity*) may be perfect for thoughtful inquirers who can handle a certain level and style of writing. Other books (like Lee Strobel's *The Case for Faith*) might have wider appeal. Some books (like Michael Brown's four volumes of *Answering Jewish Objections to Jesus* and Stan Telchin's *Betrayed*) specifically address questions Jewish people tend to ask. But some people just don't like to read books! For them, audio or video resources (like the Chosen People Ministries website www.ifoundshalom.com) may fit the bill. No one tool will suit every person or all questions.

Providing material to answer people's questions can augment your witness. But don't underestimate the power of conversation even if you're not a master apologist. You'll want to equip yourself as best as you can to start the answering process in one-on-one dialogue. The task can seem less daunting if you remember that most people tend to raise only a few common objections. Be ready to answer those questions and be willing to say, *"I don't know"* when they ask other questions. Your humility in admitting ignorance will be appreciated. And your willingness to do some research and get back to them will demonstrate respect.

We live in a time of great apologetic wealth. God has raised up many brilliant defenders of the faith who have produced rich resources to help us know what to say and how to say it. Even as new challenges emerge in "frequently asked questions" (e.g. *"Why are Christians so homophobic?"*) new resources are produced (Sam Allberry's book *Is God Anti-Gay?* is a great help on this particular question). Avail yourself of these resources. In addition to equipping you, they will also deepen your confidence in the faith you've embraced.

I like to think of answering people's questions along the lines of following a recipe. We need good ingredients and thoughtful procedures. In cooking, if you have the right ingredients but don't know how to combine them, or how hot to preheat the oven, etc., you probably won't produce anything edible. In a similar way, if we just have "answers" to questions but don't think through how to express them, we may not serve our inquiring friends as well as we should. For each of the following common questions Jewish people ask, I've provided ingredients (key components of a good answer) and suggestions for how to express the answer. I've worded the question the way some Jewish people have posed it to me.

## 1. How can you believe in a God who allows so much evil and suffering in this world, especially the evil of the Holocaust?

### Ingredients

- All worldviews have a problem with evil, not just Christianity.
- Some of those worldviews have nothing to help us when we face disease, tragedy, and death. Atheism's bankruptcy when it comes to thinking about evil is far worse than a biblical perspective, and needs to be exposed for the emptiness that it is. The same goes for agnosticism, secularism and shallow popular religion that only speaks with vague platitudes.
- Judaism and Christianity offer a framework for thinking deeply about suffering. The biblical worldview of

creation-fall-redemption-consummation offers hope and strength, even if it leaves some of our intellectual questions unanswered.

- Some prophecies of the Messiah (e.g. Isaiah 53; Psalm 16) point to his overcoming death.
- We do not have a totally satisfying answer about the problem of evil. Nobody does. But the resurrection of Jesus offers hope and joy even while you are suffering.
- While we may not know all we'd like to know about why God allows evil, we do know that some answers to this question are wrong. Views that espouse that God is not powerful enough to stop evil contradict the clear teaching of the Bible. Even Job concluded, "I know that you can do all things" (Job 42 v 2). Likewise, any view that asserts that God is uncaring or unfeeling also contradict Scripture (e.g. Psalm 103 v 11). The Messiah's atoning death and his resurrection show that God is powerful enough to overcome death and loving enough to save sinners.

### Procedures

In some ways, this question is no different from the one many people ask, whether they're Jewish or Gentile. But, for Jewish people, the reality of the Holocaust vaults this question into the realms of extreme pain and ethnic pride at the same time. You must address this question with sensitivity and empathy. Cold, distant philosophy will be (and, perhaps, should be!) dismissed out of hand. This may be an opportunity to point your Jewish friends back to Judaism on this question before offering the hope of the resurrection found in the gospel. Empathize with their pain. Admit you don't have all the answers—but the partial answer you do have is full of hope and strength. The sooner you can tell stories of believers who have handled suffering and death with hope and joy, the better. Try to move this question away from the philosophy classroom and point to the practical places in which we live. Vera Schlamm, a Holocaust survivor who came to faith in Jesus, has a particularly moving story told in her book, *Pursued*.

## 2. How can there be just one path to God? My God is more tolerant than that. All religions are just different paths up the same mountain.

### Ingredients

- There really are substantial differences between the different religions of the world. For example, Judaism teaches there is only one God while some forms of Buddhism say there is no god. This is a disagreement of core issues, not mere peripheral ones.[1]

- Judaism has always insisted on a narrow understanding of religion. The Hebrew Scriptures declare many exclusive statements similar to Isaiah's insistence, "I am God, and there is no other; I am God, and there is none like

---

1 See Stephen Prothero, *God is Not One: The Eight Rival Religions That Run the World*, HarperOne (2010), pages 2-3. Prothero is a secular scholar of religious studies with no particular religious point of view to promote. Regarding the notion that all religions are the same, he states, *"This is a lovely sentiment but it is dangerous, disrespectful, and untrue."*

me" (Isaiah 46 v 9). The history of Israel is filled with conflict between the God of Abraham, Isaac, and Jacob and other "gods" that really are not worth worshipping. The Exodus episode of the ten plagues highlights God's judgment of the false gods of Egypt.

- Jesus' claims about himself preclude the belief in numerous ways to God. While not very culturally acceptable in our "tolerant" world today, Jesus' words in John 14 v 6, "I am the way and the truth and the life. No one comes to the Father except through me" do not suffer from lack of clarity.

- The view that there really are many paths to God is a recent, mostly Western point of view that would seem odd to many people outside the West or to generations that came before us. The insistence on "many ways" is actually quite intolerant of all the religions that say their way is "the only way." Ironically, the claim of tolerance is quite intolerant.

### Procedures

Jewish people have benefitted greatly from the "all religions are the same" mantra. It has gotten a lot of would-be persecutors and proselytizers off their backs. So dismantling this cultural idol requires thoughtfulness, patience and kindness. Resist the temptation to attack this issue with sarcasm or arrogance. However, the attitudes behind this question need to be called into question and this may be painful for Jewish people. Proceed with caution but don't retreat. And don't be surprised if they get angry with you along the way. If they do, point out their "intolerance" of your perspective. Then, you can ask questions about how we can know anything. The evidence for the resurrection of Jesus can work well as a trump card. But play that card gently.

## 3. How can you say the Messiah has already come when there's no peace in our crazy world today?

### Ingredients

- The predictions of the Messiah bringing world peace come from the same Bible that tell of the Messiah atoning for sins. In fact, sometimes they come from the same prophet! (See Isaiah 2 v 2-4 and 53 v 4-6). It either means we'll have two Messiahs or one Messiah who comes twice. Even some rabbis and Jewish scholars have wondered if we might have two Messiahs to fulfill these two different kinds of prophecies.

- Christians are deeply upset about the chaos of our current world, as Jewish people are. We work diligently to eradicate suffering. And we also long for the day when the Messiah returns and brings total, worldwide peace. In the meantime, his first appearance gives us internal, individual peace in the midst of a fallen, chaotic world.

- It is tempting to give up on God's plan for the world because it doesn't seem to be progressing fast enough. One way to respond is to give up hope and turn to excessive pleasure to dull the pain from watching the way the world is going. Another response is to try to solve all the problems with human effort and no reliance on

God. Various Jewish people have resorted to both of these options but find little internal "shalom".

## Procedures

Empathize with the frustrations about the terrible state of our modern world. For all our progress, we can't seem to solve basic struggles fueled by hate, racism and violence. You'll want to do all you can to disabuse your Jewish friends of their belief that Christians only care about heaven and the hereafter, not about this world here and now. Some amount of factual reporting about Christian efforts to alleviate suffering is warranted as long as you don't spill over into bragging or overstatement.

You'll also want to show how the Bible balances human effort with dependence on God for bringing about changes in our fallen world. (Compare Micah 6 v 8 with 7 v 7.) Somewhere along the line, you might want to use an occasion like this to ask how much of the Bible they've read for themselves. This may be an opening for an invitation to read passages from the prophets together. Then, you could also explore how one of the Gospels talks about fulfillment of prophecy as well as giving instructions about how to live in our evil, fallen world.

4. You Christians believe in three gods. We Jews find that repulsive. There's only one God.

## Ingredients

- Christians also find it repulsive to believe in many gods: three or three thousand.
- Both Jews and Christians believe that there are many

things about the God revealed in the Bible that are beyond human comprehension. (See Isaiah 40 v 13-14.)

- God reveals himself in the Bible in some very clear ways and some puzzling ways. For example, God says he is the only God and worship of any other god is sin. (see Exodus 20 v 2-3). But God refers to himself in the plural in three places—Genesis 1 v 26, ("Let us make mankind in our image..."), Genesis 11 v 7 ("Come, let us go down..."), and Isaiah 6 v 8 ("And who will go for us?"). While these verses do not argue undeniably for a trinitarian God, they do allow for it and pose a question that must be answered.

- At least one Hebrew word used to describe God's oneness (*echad*) has a complex meaning that points in the direction of a plurality. Thus, in the central passage in Deuteronomy 6 v 4-9, ("The LORD is one"), the text uses the same word to describe the oneness between the man and the woman's "one flesh" in Genesis 2 v 24. There is a kind of "two in one" in marriage and a kind of "three in one" in God.

## Procedures

Don't try to prove the Trinity from Genesis 1, 11, or Isaiah 6. It may come across as begging the question. Instead, ask questions to point your Jewish friend to the realization that understanding God is beyond human reasoning. Allow for many mysteries in the Bible, of which a trinitarian view of God is just one of many aspects of God's majesty. Point out those passages where God refers to himself as "us" and allow it to be as unsettling and as challenging as it is. Don't resolve the tension just yet.

This may be a good time to introduce the concept of progressive revelation—the belief that God gradually reveals more and more truth about himself as the Scriptures unfold. In other words, we learn more about God as we read more of the Bible. God's revelation does not contradict itself but we understand more and more as we move from Moses to Malachi. This is a doctrine that both Jews and Christians adhere to.

## 5. If Jesus is the Messiah, why haven't all the rabbis recognized him? Surely they wouldn't miss someone they've been expecting for centuries.

### Ingredients

- Actually, the Jewish people have a long history of not recognizing God's prophets. It would fit rather well (but tragically) if they didn't recognize the Messiah when he followed the prophets who foretold his coming. That's the very point of Jesus' parable of the tenants (Matthew 21 v 33-46).
- Rabbis have disagreed about many, many things in Jewish history. For example, some rabbis who live in Israel today do not recognize the state of Israel as a legitimate God-ordained country because the Messiah has not yet come. Rabbis have also disagreed with each other about whether the Messiah would be a person or if we should just wait for a "messianic age" without any specific person in charge.
- The majority opinion of rabbis before the Middle Ages was that Isaiah 53 was certainly about the

Messiah. But when great persecution fell upon Jewish people from the evil actions of some who called themselves Christians, rabbis re-interpreted that and other passages so as to give less credence to Christian interpretations of the Hebrew Scriptures. In other words, circumstances dictated interpretation in place of submission to the authority of Scripture.

## Procedures

Be prepared to read, quote, paraphrase or allude to passages in Hebrew Scriptures where the people of Israel missed, mocked, or condemned the prophets God sent to them. Have some Scriptures ready to read (e.g. Ezekiel 16) but read them softly and with fear in your voice rather than haughtiness or condemnation. While you're reading these verses, remind yourself that you're included in the people referred to as "all we, like sheep, have gone astray" (Isaiah 53 v 6). Allow the power of God's word to override people's resistance to your message. The Scriptures have always had a self-authenticating nature that can cut through some terribly hardened hearts.

6. How can you believe in the virgin birth? That's just crazy. Besides, the Hebrew word in Isaiah 7 that you Christians translate as "virgin" really only means "young woman."

## Ingredients

- God does the impossible. He parted the Red Sea, poured down manna from heaven, caused the ten plagues, and on and on we could go. The God who can use Elijah to resurrect the dead (see 1 Kings 17 v 17-24) can use a virgin to conceive the Messiah.

- The "Immanuel prophecy" in Isaiah chapters 7 – 11 and its fulfillment in Matthew 1 is a complex but beautiful topic for in-depth Bible study. Regarding the specific Hebrew word *almah*, several defenses for the translation of "virgin" can be offered. It is true that the word can be translated "a young woman of marriageable age." But in ancient cultures, that always implied virginity. A "young woman of marriageable age" who was not a virgin was called a whore or some other word of condemnation. That's why the Jewish scholars who translated the Old Testament into Greek (often referred to as the Septuagint) chose a Greek word, *parthenos*, which most certainly meant a woman who had never had sex. Most pointedly (but also most confusingly), Isaiah chose a word that could be used to refer to the woman who bore the child in Isaiah 8—who served as a down payment of the prophecy as well as to Mary, a virgin, who bore Jesus. The word has enough semantic range to be used properly for both women, even though the ultimate, fullest fulfillment was reserved for Mary. The Holy Spirit inspired every word of the Scriptures in ways that cause wonder and joy.

## Procedures

If the issue at the heart of this question is the impossibility of a pregnancy without sex, you might try asking a leading question like, *"We're talking about God, right? The God who parted the Red Sea and all those other miracles*

*Jewish people have believed for centuries, right? If God can do those things, I don't see how a virgin birth is outside his skillset."* If that seems too harsh for your personality, adapt the thought to your way of saying it—the point is worth making in one way or another. This may be a place to have them embrace more deeply their Judaism and recall words from the Sabbath worship service: *"Who is like unto Thee, Oh Lord among the gods? Who is like unto Thee, glorious in holiness, fearful in praises, doing wonders?"* (see Exodus 15 v 11).

Sometimes, the virgin birth brings to the surface numerous misunderstandings that Jewish people have about the Christian faith. For example, what starts as a discussion about Mary's virginity morphs into a discussion about the incarnation. They may say, *"You Christians think Jesus became God. That's ridiculous."* Our response begins with a correction. *"We don't think Jesus became God. We believe God became a man."* And then we can ask a question that raises the possibility of that belief. *"If God wanted to take on human form, that wouldn't be too difficult for him, would it?"* Sometimes, the discussion of the virgin birth leads to discussions of Roman Catholic beliefs about Mary's perpetual virginity, etc. On numerous occasions, I've had to distinguish Protestant views from Roman Catholic ones and appeal to the Bible, and only the Bible, as the source of truth. This takes some time.

We could go on but these are the most frequently asked questions I've come across. Prepare to respond to these and you'll be equipped for more than 90% of the intellectual challenges you'll face.

But there is one more question that deserves special attention. It's the unspoken question that may lurk behind all the others. No matter how convinced some Jewish people might be that Jesus really is the Messiah and that they must trust him for salvation, they may continue to refuse to take that step of faith. Many Gentile Christians have been baffled and bothered by this and, in some cases, have expressed their exasperation. But you must sense the difficulty Jewish people experience when they get to this point. Their head tells them one thing and their heart tells them another. Their individual intellect cannot deny that Jesus is who he claimed to be. But their communal loyalty makes them feel like a traitor. Their connection to family, friends, and their people is something deeper than ethnicity, race and religion combined. And this isn't paranoia or overstatement.

Thus, at some point in conversation with your Jewish friend, you may have to say something like this:

> I imagine this must be a very difficult discussion for you. I won't pretend to understand how this may be effecting you. But are you willing to seek the truth no matter how uncomfortable it may be? Are you willing to ask God to guide you into the truth no matter how great the cost?

Say these words with a soft voice and direct eye-contact. Let your friend know you care about them and about the truth.

# Joseph's story

Soccer was Joseph's god. It brought him adulation from a lot of people, offered a great distraction from the pain of his parents' divorce, and even provided a certain amount of financial security when he received a full scholarship for all four years of college. Life was good for him as a college freshman at a prestigious school that didn't cost him a penny. Perhaps life was a bit too good. Less than a year after enrolling, he found himself sent home from college due to poor academic grades. It's tough to maintain the necessary grades when you're going to more parties than classes.

Without the scholarship, he needed a job, and the only work he could find was rigorous manual labor lugging bricks for a bricklayer. His body was ideal for the soccer field but inadequate for the demands of a construction sight. He felt humiliated and broken.

His construction foreman intrigued Joseph because he was always so joyful—even while doing such hard work. One day the foreman gathered the whole crew around him and gave each man a small pamphlet. Joseph guessed it was about Jesus and he was right. Most of the men threw the tract on the ground but Joseph stuck it in his pocket, not wanting to appear rude. He didn't read it. But he didn't throw it away either. Even though he was Jewish, Joseph kept an open mind and figured he'd get around to reading it one day.

One week later the foreman asked him if he had read the booklet and Joseph felt compelled to tell the truth—no, he had not. Kindly but firmly, the foreman asked him to give it a read and tell him what he thought. So he did. He remembers the title of the pamphlet as *The Reality and Remedy for Sin.*

"I read it and I didn't understand it," Joseph recalls. "At the end of the booklet, it said, 'If you do not understand this, read it again!' So I read it over and over and, suddenly, I realized that booklet was right! I was a sinner and I needed a sacrifice for my sins. That's where my Jewishness kicked in. The need for a sacrifice for sin made a lot of sense."

What the booklet said about Jesus was tough for Joseph to accept. But so much of the rest of the booklet seemed so true and so convicting that he asked the God of Abraham, Isaac, and Jacob to show him whether it was true that Jesus was the Messiah. "When I prayed that, God answered. He made it so clear that only by accepting Jesus' death on the cross for my sins could I be made holy and enter into a relationship with God."

Decades later, Joseph still feels amazed at how God chose to use an ordinary guy who was bold enough to hand out a tract and persistent enough to ask if that tract was ever read. A co-worker sowed seeds and God chose to water them.

# Chapter six

# Speaking with wisdom

Time for another Yiddish word: *sachel* (rhymes with "playful"). Like most Yiddish words, it's difficult to define. The closest English word might be wisdom. But it's a particular kind of wisdom—a kind of "street-smarts" or native good sense or intuition or practical judgment. A person with *sachel* knows what to say and how to say it. Evangelism takes *sachel*.

Of course, evangelism involves far more than that. It's energized by prayer, grounded in the Scriptures, streams across webs of friendship, benefits from injections of apologetics, requires total dependence on the Holy Spirit, and flows best through expressions of compassion and kindness.

But without *sachel* or wisdom, our words easily fall upon deaf ears. Much evangelism lacks sensitivity and, while theologically sound and apologetically watertight, comes across as socially awkward, emotionally weird, or downright disrespectful. We would all do well to consider how we communicate as well as what we communicate. Here are some practical considerations (in no particular order) about engaging Jewish people in wise ways so as to express God's love with more than just words.

- Ultimately, you're trying to introduce Jewish people to a person—the wise, astounding, wonder-full Jewish person of Jesus, the Messiah. Begin in a variety of ways, talking about a variety of topics (faith, God, how life can make sense, why things are messed up, why we are messed up, meaning or purpose in life, etc.) but, eventually, **talk about Jesus and why you love him**, how great it is to know him, and how he has made a difference in your life.

- Along these same lines, **tell your story and emphasize how good the gospel is.** To be sure, you want to say why you believe the gospel message is true. But you also want to share *why* it's good. How has your saving faith, based on the atoning work of a savior on a cross all those many years ago, made you a better person, spouse, parent, friend, etc.? How has the grace of the gospel made you kinder, more peaceful, happier, and not afraid of the future? The more specific you can be, the better. It's one thing to say, *"My faith helps me a lot."* It's better to say, *"The fact that my wife and I have received forgiveness from God has made it easier for us to forgive each other. Without that, we would have split a long time ago."*

- **It's OK to be Gentile.** I know that sounds odd but a lot of Gentile Christians have felt unqualified to witness to Jewish people. But most Jewish believers in Jesus say they were led to faith, primarily, by Gentiles. Should you try to introduce your Jewish friend to a Jewish believer you know? *Sure.* But not right away. Or not as an absolute requirement. The heart of the gospel message declares this good news is for both Jews and Gentiles because all people, Jews and Gentiles, need it.

- **Don't rush. But don't relax either.** How I wish I could offer a standard timetable for all conversion processes! Jewish people have a lot of obstacles, both intellectual and emotional, to overcome in moving from unbelief to salvation. We want all evangelism to go from a dead stop to full speed in less than ten seconds, as if we only need to step on the gas and get to cruising speed immediately. But a lot of evangelism feels more like stepping on the gas and then easing up, speeding up and then slowing down, shifting gears and making sure not to crash. This takes time, sensitivity to the Holy Spirit's leading, and listening for clues (verbal and non-verbal) to see how your friend is progressing.

- **Be ready for surprises.** Some of your Jewish friends identify strongly with their religion. Others may know absolutely nothing about their Bible, their history or traditions. And some fall somewhere in between. Assume little. Ask much. Listen carefully.

- **Define your terms.** And choose them carefully. Avoid the word "convert" and speak instead of "believing in the Messiah." Some phrases work well for some people. Others miss the mark. If you do speak of "Messianic Jews" or "completed Jews" or "Jewish believers," be ready to explain what you mean. The whole concept of being Jewish and Christian seems like the ultimate oxymoron to Jewish people. Don't express it in a matter-of-fact way. If anything, express it while acknowledging the oddness of the expression. *"I know this might seem like a contradiction but I really believe you can believe in Jesus and still be Jewish. In fact, I think it would fulfill your Jewishness."*

- **Don't blend religion with politics.** Most Jewish people side with liberal causes and might think of conservatives in some pretty ugly ways. They don't need to convert to conservative political perspectives in order to be saved by Jesus. This may be more of a problem in parts of America than in other parts of the world, but implying that faith in the Messiah must also change their voting patterns adds an unnecessary stumbling block to an already difficult process.

- **Resist the temptation to start the process by asking, *"How do Jewish people get forgiveness for sins since the temple is no longer standing?"*** It's amazing how common this approach is. And it's equally amazing how bad it is. It's a non-starter so don't start with it. In fact, I suggest eliminating the question completely from your conversations about forgiveness. For most Jewish people, the temple was how God worked "back then" and now he works differently. This doesn't bother Jewish people at all and they really can't understand why Christians get so worked up about it. In fact, the entire modern Jewish world was launched and transformed after the destruction of the temple when, as one prominent rabbi stated, *"We have a means for making atonement. And what is it? It is deeds of love…"*

- **But don't give up on the topic of forgiveness as a starting point for discussion.** It may be the best ways to talk about the gospel. Even though Judaism teaches a great deal about forgiveness, for most Jewish people it seldom becomes an experiential reality. They fast, pray, and confess all day long on *Yom Kippur* and hear words about God's lovingkindness at weddings and funerals but, as the writer of Hebrews put it, "…without the shedding of blood there is no forgiveness" (Hebrews 9 v 22). Believers in Jesus have a substantive basis for forgiveness—the finished work of the cross. Sometimes we tend to take the once-for-all-ness of the gospel for granted or forget its power. But Jewish people who don't know of the Messiah's substitutionary atonement cannot experience the freedom found there. Find ways to express how that freedom works in your life today and connect your current experience to the event of the cross.

- **Reading about Jesus on the internet is safe and anonymous.** You'd be amazed at how many unsaved Jewish people spend time visiting websites that proclaim the gospel. Point them there. Put links on your Facebook page. Find resources that would not seem cheesy, pushy, weird or mean, and tell your Jewish friends about them.

- **Jewish people like to read.** But you probably shouldn't just give them a book in too casual a way. It'll seem awkward and they may just feel bad about reading what you give them. Ask if they'd be willing to read something you've found interesting. If they seem OK about that, lend them the book and say you'd like to discuss it when they're finished. They can hang on to it for a long time but a loan is different than a gift. In ways that may seem counterintuitive, a loaned book may serve the process of their coming to faith better in the long run. Alternatively, if you really want to give them a special book as a gift, then wrap it in nice paper and present it to them with a card and an expression of how much you value their friendship.

- **Don't tell Jewish jokes, especially ones about money.** At the same time, don't be surprised if *they* tell you Jewish jokes. It'll be awkward. Practice your best polite smile while not laughing too hard. If your friendship progresses to the point of your being able to tell some jokes, that will build your credibility— unless you're really not good at telling jokes. Jewish people have little patience for bad comedians.
- There is no substitute for one-on-one Bible study.

# Chapter seven

# Connecting with the body of Messiah

Judaism and Christianity are simultaneously individual and communal religions. Each individual person needs to embrace the faith and live out that faith in community. Generally speaking, Judaism tends to emphasize the community more than the individual. Christianity (at least, as it is often practiced today) tends to emphasize the individual more than the community. The sharp dichotomy comes when you consider that no one is born a Christian. We believe everyone needs to be "born again." From the Jewish perspective, if you're born into a Jewish family, you're Jewish. *"I was born a Jew and I'll die a Jew"* are words most Jewish people have said and meant rather sincerely.

Part of the task of helping your Jewish friend understand the gospel includes clarifying this difference. You can be "born a Jew" but you can't be born a Christian. And you can be "born a Jew", believe in Jesus the Messiah, and still be Jewish.

Not only is the Christian faith a communal faith but, for many people, being born again is a communal experience. I don't mean that people get saved in groups—although that certainly does happen, as the salvation of three thousand people recorded in Acts 2 displays. But I'm referring to the common experience that people come to faith by connecting with a group of believers, hearing a variety of stories, and watching how people live out their faith in community. A crucial part of the process of witnessing to your Jewish friend involves bringing them to church.

This is easier said than done. You could bring them to your church but that might have some problems. Or you could accompany them to a Messianic Jewish congregation but that might have some problems. There are no problem-free solutions, but don't let that stop you from inviting them to connect to the larger body of Messiah.

Regarding churches, you must realize that every church expresses the faith in culturally saturated ways. There are no "culturally neutral" expressions of worship. Every song, every liturgical recitation, every word comes across as Western or Asian or British or German or Caucasian or Jewish or Gentile. This does not mean that you must avoid all Gentile-dominated churches as places for your Jewish friend to visit. It just means you'll want to hear their thoughts about the entire experience, not just the doctrine that was proclaimed.

At the risk of drawing some hard lines, I do not think it is wise to invite Jewish people to Roman Catholic or liberal Protestant churches. In numerous ways, all of which are bad, these churches add unnecessary stumbling blocks to the process of clarifying the gospel to Jewish people. And if your church takes a strong stand against the nation of Israel for whatever reason... well, I hope you'll see why that's a huge problem—for them and for you!

## Messianic congregations

Visiting a Messianic Jewish congregation might work as a way for your Jewish friend to feel culturally and religiously at home while still encountering the person of Jesus. I have been a part of one thriving congregation and visited many others, and found them to be wonderful expressions of gospel faith that feel "right" to my Jewish background.

These congregations sing songs with Hebraic or Israeli melodies, recite prayers from Jewish traditions and from the book of Psalms, and preach sermons that link Old and New Testament texts. They have no pipe organs and never sing songs written by Martin Luther. When I first visited one as a new believer and heard music that resonated with my Jewish bones, I almost wept tears of joy.

But, just like all churches, Messianic congregations are not without their problems. Just as there are churches you should avoid because of bad doctrine or poor discipleship, so too with Messianic congregations. You'll probably want to visit a congregation before inviting your unsaved friend there. Be discerning. Consider all the many warnings we get in Scripture about testing the spirits (1 John 4 v 1) and rejecting "whatever else is contrary to the sound doctrine that conforms to the gospel" (1 Timothy 1 v 10-11).

Yet again, I feel the need to repeat something about the intersection of our efforts and God's sovereignty. Evangelism occurs at the mysterious and beautiful intersection of human activity and divine power. We say words, invite to gatherings, suggest things to read, ask questions, express concern. And as we do these things, God does what only he can do—raises the dead, opens blind eyes, and convicts of sin. Don't obsess in ways that assume you're in charge of the entire process. You're not. Step into the process of engaging with Jewish people, understanding their world, and sharing good news, and watch God do the impossible.

# Conclusion

# The feast

If you've ever had the profound pleasure of participating in a Passover *Seder* (the ceremonial meal), you know the depth of connection between the old covenant and the new, the links between the Exodus and the Messiah's Last Supper, and how God's deliverance of Israel out of physical bondage foreshadowed his mighty work of salvation out of spiritual bondage. You rejoice in deeper ways when you remember, *"Messiah, our Passover Lamb, has been sacrificed"* (1 Corinthians 5 v 7).

There is an oral tradition about the Passover meal which says that the last thing you were supposed to eat was a piece of lamb, the main course. Allowing that taste to linger in your mouth would prolong the celebration of freedom and help you meditate longer on all that God did those many years ago. The lamb, as the central symbol of the *Seder*, pointed back to the lamb that was slain and whose blood was spread on the doorposts outside the Jewish slaves' dwellings.

Then, when God poured out his wrath on the Egyptians and their false gods through the tenth and final plague—the slaying of the first born—he would "pass over" the houses of those covered by the blood. Putting the blood on the doorposts outwardly displayed their inward faith in God—a faith that would save them.

But when Jesus celebrated the Passover *Seder* with his disciples—Jewish men who had participated in *Seders* many times before—he broke with tradition and took bread... after they had eaten the last piece of lamb. He wanted the sacrifice of his body to linger in their memories even more than the sacrifice of the lamb. His death would fulfill the picture of the death of the lamb. He would provide the means for God's wrath to "pass over" them. The greater deliverance through the greater sacrifice deserved greater lingering, meditation and wonder.

As you come to the end of this book, I want the taste of the gospel to linger in your hearts and minds. I want you to taste and see that Jesus is the one who fulfills all the incomplete pictures in the stories of the Old Testament. He satisfies the longings that were raised but then disappointed by all the key characters of the Bible. And he is the one your Jewish friends long for. He is the one the law prepares them for, the one the prophets point them to, and the one their feasts anticipate.

I want you to remember the inseparable connections between the Hebrew Scriptures and the new-covenant Scriptures because, when you begin conversations with Jewish people, they may seem more like "enemies" of the gospel (see Romans 11 v 28) than like "God's chosen people." A few snippets of Jewish believers' stories may help.

One Jewish friend, who now believes in Jesus and

leads a Messianic congregation, loves to tell how he first responded to the gospel. As a manager of a delicatessen, he had to be trained in the fine art of slicing lox (preserved salmon). The instructor weaved gospel preaching in between instructions of knife techniques. Finally, my friend could stand these uninvited sermonettes no longer and told him, "to take his gospel and stick it where the salmon waste goes."

Another Jewish friend saw how his wife had been transformed when her faith came alive as a result of attending a Bible study. When that group chose to study Genesis, he thought it was safe to go because, as he tells it, *"I intended to study Genesis since I thought I wouldn't have to confront Jesus or the New Testament. I could not have been more wrong! These Christians see Jesus on every page."* As he read and studied, he became captivated by Jesus and his wise teaching. On a business trip, alone in a hotel room, he opened a drawer of the nightstand next to the bed, took out a Bible placed there by the Gideons, and opened to the genealogy at the beginning of Matthew's Gospel. He was struck by how familiar all those names were and the inseparability of Old and New Testaments. He became a believer later that day.

My father, who was mad at God for decades because of the evil he had seen while fighting in World War II, vowed never to believe in Jesus the way two of his sons, his wife, and several friends did. But over time, accompanying my mother to worship services at a Messianic congregation, hearing the gospel week after week, he softened. Well after turning 80 years old, he attended a Passover *Seder* hosted by that congregation and heard again about Yeshua as the ultimate lamb. He became a believer that evening and found *shalom* in ways he couldn't find elsewhere. He requested we sing *Amazing Grace* at his funeral, which we did shortly after his 90th birthday.

At the end of the *Seder* Jesus celebrated with his disciples, we read:

> And when He had taken a cup and given thanks, He gave it to them, saying, "Drink from it, all of you; for this is My blood of the covenant, which is poured out for many for forgiveness of sins. "But I say to you, I will not drink of this fruit of the vine from now on until that day when I drink it new with you in My Father's kingdom." **Matthew 26 v 27-29**

We live in between the time Jesus gave that cup and the time when he returns to drink it anew. It's a time of waiting. It's also a time of proclaiming. We wait while we proclaim the best news ever—to the Jew first and to everyone else who will gather in that "great multitude that no one could count, from every nation, tribe, people and language, standing before the throne and before the Lamb" (Revelation 7 v 9).

# Resources

## Understanding Judaism and Jewish people

**Thomas Cahill,**
*The Gifts of the Jews: How a Tribe of Desert Nomads Changed the Way Everyone Thinks and Feels.*

**Paul Johnson,**
*A History of the Jews.*

**Chaim Potok,**
*Wanderings: Chaim Potok's History of the Jews; The Chosen; The Promise.*

**Herman Wouk,**
*This is My God.*

## Understanding biblical connections

**Darrell Bock and Mitch Glaser,** *To the Jew First: The Case for Jewish Evangelism in Scripture and History.*

**Michael L. Brown,**
*Answering Jewish Objections to Jesus (4 Volumes); Our Hands are Stained with Blood.*

**Alfred Edersheim,** *The Life and Times of Jesus the Messiah.*

**Mitch and Zhava Glaser,**
*The Fall Feasts of Israel.*

**Walter Kaiser,** *The Messiah in the Old Testament.*

**Moishe and Ceil Rosen,**
*Christ in the Passover.*

**Michael Rydelnik,**
*The Messianic Hope: Is the Hebrew Bible Really Messianic?*

**Stan Telchin,**
*Abandoned: What is God's Will for the Jewish People and the Church?*

**Martha Zimmerman,**
*Celebrating Biblical Feasts: In Your Home or Church.*

## Books to help with Jewish evangelism

**Greg Koukl,**
*Tactics: A Game Plan for Discussing Your Christian Convictions.*

**Randy Newman,**
*Questioning Evangelism: Engaging People's Hearts the Way Jesus Did; Bringing the Gospel Home: Witnessing to Family Members, Close Friends, and Others Who Know You Well.*

**Moishe and Ceil Rosen,**
*Witnessing to Jews: Practical Ways to Relate the Love of Jesus.*

**Barry Rubin,**
*You Bring the Bagels, I'll Bring the Gospel: Sharing the Messiah With Your Jewish Neighbor.*

**Mitch Glaser,**
*Isaiah 53 Explained: This Chapter May Change Your Life.*

**Vera Schlamm with Bob Friedman,**
*Pursued.*

**Stan Telchin,**
*Betrayed!*

## Evangelistic books to give to Jewish friends

**Arnold Fruchtenbaum and Joni Prinjinski,**
*Jesus Was a Jew.*

## Websites

**www.chosenpeople.com**

**www.jewsforjesus.org**

# Other titles in this series

## Engaging with Hindus
### by Robin Thomson

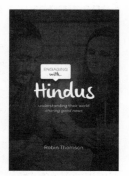

Hindism is the third largest faith in the world, and yet many Christians know very little about Hindu beliefs and lifestyle

This short book is designed to help both Christians and whole churches understand more about Hindus, and to reach out to them with the good news of the gospel.

**Robin Thomson** spent twenty years in India teaching the Bible and training church leaders. He is the author of several books relating the Bible to Asian culture.

## Engaging with Atheists
### by David Robertson

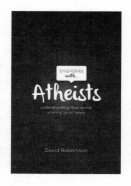

Many Christians are fearful of engaging in conversation with atheists—believing that they will be hostile to Christian beliefs and conversations about the Bible.

This short book is designed to help both Christians and whole churches understand more about the questions and issues that atheists of various kinds have about Christian faith, and to reach out to them with the good news of the gospel.

**David Robertson** is the minister of St Peter's Free Church in Dundee, Scotland, and a director of the Solas Centre for Public Christianity. He is the author of *The Dawkins Letters*, and has publicly debated Richard Dawkins and other prominent atheists throughout the UK and Europe.

# Other titles in this series

## Engaging with Muslims
by John Klaassen

Many Christians in the west are fearful of engaging in conversations about their faith with Muslims—believing that they will be hostile to Christian beliefs and discussions about the Bible.

This short book is designed to help both Christians and whole churches understand more about the variety of Muslims there are living in the West, and to reach out to them with the good news of the gospel. Written at a level that everyone can understand, this book emphasizes the importance of forming loving relationships—something that all Christians are able to do.

**John Klaassen** is Associate Professor of Global Studies at Boyce College, in Louisville Kentucky, USA. Previously he worked in relief and development in North Africa. John is married and has two children.

> *"For some time now there has been a desperate need for a practical guide to assist Western pastors and church leaders in equipping their congregations for effective ministry among their Muslim neighbors. Filled with helpful illustrations, conversion stories, and questions for further reflection, Engaging with Muslims is the place to begin for those who are serious both about understanding their Muslim neighbors and reaching them with the gospel."*
>
> **Dr J. Scott Bridger**
> Director of the Jenkins Center for
> the Christian Understanding of Islam

www.thegoodbook.com | .co.uk | .com.au | .co.nz

**Q**uestions
Christians ask

*An excellent series for building your own faith, and helping others discover the Christian message for themselves*

## Is God anti-gay?
### by Sam Allberry

Christians, the church and the Bible seem to be out of step with modern attitudes toward homosexuality.

In this short, simple book, Sam Allberry wants to help confused Christians understand what God has said about these questions in the Scriptures, and he offers a positive and liberating way forward through the debate.

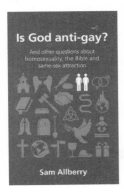

## Can I really trust the Bible?
### by Barry Cooper

The Bible makes big claims for itself. But do those claims stand up? Aren't the stories just legends? Hasn't the information been corrupted over time? Isn't the Bible full of mistakes? And isn't it culturally outdated?

In this absorbing little book, Barry Cooper explores these questions —and many others— with warmth, wit and integrity.

www.thegoodbook.com | .co.uk | .com.au | .co.nz

the**good**book
COMPANY

# thegoodbook
## COMPANY
*Opening up the Bible*

At The Good Book Company, we are dedicated to helping Christians and local churches grow. We believe that God's growth process always starts with hearing clearly what he has said to us through his timeless word—the Bible.

Ever since we opened our doors in 1991, we have been striving to produce resources that honor God in the way the Bible is used. We have grown to become an international provider of user-friendly resources to the Christian community, with believers of all backgrounds and denominations using our Bible studies, books, evangelistic resources, DVD-based courses and training events.

We want to equip ordinary Christians to live for Christ day by day, and churches to grow in their knowledge of God, their love for one another, and the effectiveness of their outreach.

Call us for a discussion of your needs or visit one of our local websites for more information on the resources and services we provide.

Your friends at The Good Book Company

---

**NORTH AMERICA**
**UK & EUROPE**
**AUSTRALIA**
**NEW ZEALAND**

thegoodbook.com
thegoodbook.co.uk
thegoodbook.com.au
thegoodbook.co.nz

866 244 2165
0333 123 0880
(02) 6100 4211
(+64) 3 343 2463

**WWW.CHRISTIANITYEXPLORED.ORG**
Our partner site is a great place for those exploring the Christian faith, with a clear explanation of the good news, powerful testimonies and answers to difficult questions.